Pricing in Theory and Practice

Pricing in Theory and Practice

Bjarke Fog

HANDELSHØJSKOLENS FORLAG
Distribution: Munksgaard International Publishers Ltd
Copenhagen

© Handelshøjskolens Forlag 1994
Set in Plantin by Grafisk Værk A/S, Denmark
Printed in Denmark by Reproset, Copenhagen 1994
Cover designed by Kontrapunkt
Book designed by Jørn Ekstrøm

ISBN 87-16-13229-7

Series A
COPENHAGEN STUDIES IN ECONOMICS AND MANAGEMENT, NO. 2

Preface

Most students of economic theory have felt the lack of harmony between price theory and the way prices are set in practice. The subject of this book is the relation between pricing in theory and in reality.

The book is planned neither as an ordinary textbook on managerial economics nor as one on price theory, of which there are already a great number of excellent examples in existence. Instead it has been written to respond to a need which I, personally, have always felt has not been fulfilled. It is meant to be a supplementary book, based on the assumption that the reader is already familiar with elementary theory, but is interested in how to apply the theory to problems in practice.

I have ventured to write the text in English myself, although I am fully aware that my command of the language is far from perfect. Fortunately I have had the benefit of assistance from two persons who have English as their mother tongue. Nicolai Holt has tried to correct my language in a preliminary draft and John Murphy has done his best to transform my version of the English language in this edition. To both of them I extend my sincere thanks.

I also want to thank the secretaries of our institute, Sannie Fiil, Sena Filekovic, Fritze Lundstrom, Birgitte Rekalos, Anje Schmidt and Anni Vagner, for their help in preparing the manuscript.

Bjarke Fog

Contents

Introduction 9

1. **Normative and Descriptive Theories**
   The distinction between two types of theories 17
   Problems of a descriptive theory 18
   Research problems 19
   Classification of theories 20

2. **Marginalism as a Normative Theory**
   The content of marginalism 24
   Presentation of the theory 30
   Relevant cost information 33
   Cost information for optimum pricing 35
   Implications for practice 37

3. **Marginalism as a Descriptive Theory**
   Statement of the problem 43
   Explanation of relative prices 47
   Reaction to changes 50
   Effects of taxes and subsidies 51
   Conclusion 56

4. **Full Cost as a Descriptive Theory**
   Definition of full cost 59
   The content of full cost 60
   The existence of full cost 64
   Illustrative examples 66
   Rules of thumb 70
   The controversy between marginalism and full cost 73
   A general descriptive theory? 77
   Efficient prices 81

5. **Full Cost as a Normative Theory**
   The merits of full cost 85
   Illustrative examples 87
   Advantages and disadvantages of full cost pricing 90

6. **Price Strategy in Competitive Environments**
   Different types of competition 93
   Illustrative cases 95
   Oligopoly theory as a descriptive theory 100
   Oligopoly and game theory 105

The theory of joint profit maximization   109
Oligopoly theory as a normative theory   113
Pricing under monopolistic competition   115

7. Multi-product Pricing
Joint production   120
Multiple products   124

8. Transfer Pricing
Definition   129
Transfer pricing in theory and practice   131
The practical solution   137
The theoretical solution   137

9. Price Discrimination
Conditions for price discrimination   139
Price discrimination in practice   140
Predatory pricing   140
Discount policy   142
Charging for extras   145

10. Vertical Relations
The basic theory   147
Examples of monopsony   148
Subcontracting   151
Relations between producers and retailers   152

11. Conclusion   158

References   163

Index   167

Introduction

Theories about price have always constituted an important and integral part of general economic theory. Price theories can be understood in a number of ways. A fundamental distinction is between the macroeconomic and microeconomic perspectives on price.

The macroeconomic perspective takes a view of the whole economy and focuses on the general price level. The aim of the macroeconomic perspective is to explain how prices are formed, why prices change and why some change more than others.

Microeconomic theory focuses on the individual firm or seller. It attempts to explain all the problems connected with the determination of specific prices in specific firms.

A question that has always attracted interest is whether existing theories are realistic. Discussion of this subject has often been rather heated and never seems able to end. Part of the controversy arises from the fact that it is not always explained what "realistic" means. Another reason is due to the inexact use of various terms. Such concepts as profit maximization, demand function and marginal cost may have a precise meaning in a theoretical model but not always in a real situation.

It is therefore essential in any presentation that the terminology be clear from the beginning. This book is driven by a key distinction between normative and descriptive theory. A normative theory constitutes a guide to the decision-maker on how to achieve a chosen objective. The goal may be maximization of profit, and the price that satisfies this goal is called the optimum price.[1] Thus, the aim of the theory is to instruct the decision-maker on how to determine the optimum price under given assumptions. It may be applied to any goal that can be specified sufficiently clearly. Thus, if the chosen goal is to obtain a specific market share, the objective for a normative theory is to determine the price that will realize that goal.

The use of the words normative and descriptive may create difficulties for english-speaking readers. First, a more conventional distinction is between normative and positive theories. Second, a theory can be conceived as being normative in the sense that it arises from an assessment about what the most important goal ought to be (maximizing welfare, maximizing growth, etc.). Thus, the word normative can be understood in a moral or ethical sense: what ought to be the solution? However, the word normative as used here indicates what the price should be to achieve a chosen objective, for example, profit maximization, but

---

[1] But even this concept, the optimum price, is ambiguous. For example, we may distinguish between short-term optimum and long-term optimum; optima under different assumptions as to competitor reactions, etc. Thus, in a specific situation, there is not necessarily one and only one optimum price.

not what it ought to be in a moral sense. The normative theory is of interest to the decision-maker and thus is applied inside the firm.

In contrast, a descriptive price theory is viewed from the outside. The theory has as its aim to explain why prices are set as they are. Thus, in principle, it is a descriptive theory when an economist explains that the reason why a specific brand of beer costs 1.5 dollars is because the brewery believes that the price elasticity is 2 and because marginal costs are 75 cents.[2]

In this situation, there is no difference between a normative and a descriptive theory.

In general, there would be no difference between normative and descriptive theories if: (a) they were based on the same assumptions, (b) the objectives were the same, (c) there were perfect information and (d) business executives always acted rationally. However, these conditions are rarely fulfilled, and I will demonstrate that there are differences between normative and descriptive theories.

The presentation of microeconomic theory in basic textbooks is usually normative. It is based on assumptions of profit maximization and perfect information and concentrates on determining the theoretically optimum price. The presentation often contains descriptive elements in the form of illustrative examples from practice. The main concern of the theory is to determine an equilibrium price. Thus, the Cournot model constitutes an equilibrium because it solves the oligopoly output problem, which is an equilibrium in the sense that none of the oligopolists have a motive to deviate from this equilibrium – under the stated assumptions. But it does not determine the absolute maximum joint profit, as collusion gives an even better result.

These elementary normative models are often used as a basis for a descriptive theory. Explicitly or implicitly, the assumption is made that the models also give a fair description of pricing in the real world. But if this assumption is not fulfilled, the inevitable result is that descriptive economic theories based on normative models become unrealistic. This criticism can be raised against a great number of the models within welfare economics. The models simply start by assuming that existing prices are the optimum ones! But if this is not the case, the models are no more realistic than the assumptions on which they are based.

Thus, oligopoly models are often based on the Cournot solution. You simply start by assuming that the Cournot solution is realized. But the Cournot model is naive and totally unrealistic. It certainly has its value as a purely theoretical model but is useless in any descriptive theory.

In 1960, I published the results of an empirical study of pricing policies used by Danish manufacturers.[3] I interviewed representatives of 139

---

[2]Because the condition p= marginal cost $\frac{e}{e-1}$ is fullfilled.

[3]B. Fog. Industrial pricing policies. Amsterdam, North-Holland Publishing Company. A great number of economists have made similar studies. Just to mention a few:
  back:

Danish industrial firms. I used the information obtained, supplemented with other available material, as the basis for a comparison of traditional, normative price theory with pricing in practice.

I am now returning to the same subject, but this time from a different angle. In the first study I was an outside observer trying to get insight into the pricing process. For the last 30 years I have taken an active part in pricing decisions and my observations are now a view from the inside.

I have been a member of the board of directors of six companies (and chairman of the board of one), most fairly large by Danish standards. For example, in one of them, all important price changes were discussed by the manager and myself. Further, I have acted as a consultant to a number of companies with regard to their pricing policies.

To avoid misunderstanding, I shall explain what is the purpose of this book – and what it is not. It is not an attempt to present a general descriptive price theory. I have been tempted to do this but found the task too ambitious. It would require that I systematically supplement my own examples with cases from the literature. This would have been especially necessary on a great number of subjects in which I have no personal experience. However, I have deliberately chosen to limit myself to a presentation based on my own impressions. Thus, a number of pricing problems are not even mentioned in this book, such as the kinked demand curve, pricing through a product's life cycle, pricing in a market strategy and pricing under perfect competition.

Neither is this presentation a book on normative pricing in the form of a systematic and instructive guide of how to set prices in a rational way. Naturally, when working in practice I have tried to apply the theory and realized its advantages and felt its shortcomings. Only rarely have I used a specific model. But I fully realize that my theoretical knowledge has influenced my way of thinking. I believe that it would have been possible for me to write a purely normative textbook based on these experiences, but that would have been a different book. In my opinion, excellent presentations of the simplified basic theory do exist.[4] But the problem is that many business executives consider the economic models to be oversimplified and too remote from reality to be of practical use. The normative theory should be developed further, accompanied by more realistic assumptions. First, a guide is needed as to how to apply the theoretical principles when you have imperfect information. Here I primarily focus on the descriptive theory, because I find the descriptive theory, in its present stage of development, absolutely unsatis-

back: *The pricing of manufactures* (1964), D.C. Hague: *Economic theory and business behaviour* (1949), D.C. Hague: *Pricing in business* (1971), Kaplan, Dirlam and Lanzilotti: *Pricing in big business* (1958), G.J. Stigler and J. Kindahl: *The behaviour of industrial prices* (1970), P Sylos-Labini: *Industrial pricing in the United Kingdom* (1979), R.C. Skinner: *The determination of selling prices* (1970), J.F. Pearce: *A study in price policy* (1956).

[4] For example, Arthur Marshall: *More profitable pricing*. London, 1980. Kent B. Monroe: *Pricing. Making profitable decisions*. New York, 1979.

factory. My main purpose has been to contribute to the development of a more realistic descriptive price theory.

A descriptive theory has to be based on knowledge of how prices are actually determined. The relevant information can originate from different sources. Examples of price policy are often mentioned in newspapers, periodicals and company reports. Information on pricing may also be revealed in studies of specific industries, even though pricing may not be the central object. Thus, government investigations of specific trades often contain valuable information. The main theme may be, for example, the degree of competitiveness – or lack of it – within a trade, but the report will invariably throw light on pricing processes.

But the main source of information has always been empirical investigations, with the specific objective of obtaining insight into the pricing process. The easiest and most direct approach is to use mailed questionnaires.[5] The value of this method is limited. It may give some general basic information, but for such a complicated problem as whether actual prices agree with the theory, the method is too superficial. It focuses on the formal procedure and expects the theoretical models to be directly observable in actual business situations.[6] I can imagine what would happen if I were asked to complete a questionnaire in one of the companies I worked for. I am absolutely convinced that, no matter how experienced I was, how honest I was, and how well the questionnaire was constructed, they would never get a correct impression of how the price was set.

Information obtained through personal interviews is more reliable. But the difficulties are great. The interviewer cannot always take the responses at face value but has to interpret them. One danger is that the people interviewed respond by saying what they ought to do – not what they actually do. The risk is not openly false answers but that the respondents try to give an idealized picture.[7]

[5] The first – and maybe for that reason – most well known was the research by Hall and Hitch (R.L. Hall and C.J. Hitch: *Price theory and business behaviour*. Oxford Economic Papers, 1939) Also later researchers have used questionnaires. Thus, for Great Britain Skinner conducted an analysis in 1968 in which questionnaires were sent to all members of the Merseyside Chamber of Commerce. (R.C. Skinner: "The determination of selling prices", *Journal of Industrial Economics*, 1970). This was followed by a study of Atkins and Skinner, which was unique as the questionnaires were mailed to marketing directors rather than managing directors.(B. Atkin and R. Skinner: "How British industry prices", *Industrial Market Research*, 1975,)
In the United States, questionnaires have been used by Earley. The questionnaires were mailed to the companies rated as "excellently managed" by the American Institute of Management. (J.S. Earley: "Marginal policies of 'excellently managed' companies", *American Economic Review*, 1956.)
[6] Dorward makes the following comment on the use of questionnaires: "Hall and Hitch (1939), as well as others such as Barback (1964) , seem to have fallen into the trap of equating marginalism with explicit textbook marginalist behavior. This caused them to ignore, or at least play down, the ample evidence of implicit marginalism provided by their businessmen, when departing from the full-cost price under pressure of market forces." Neil Dorward: *Pricing decisions*, p 99.

Thus: "In theory I should determine the price as total average cost plus a normal profit, because that constitutes a fair price, but due to the competitive situation I have to accept a lower price." In spite of all possible pitfalls, this method will probably be the main future source for gaining insight into the pricing process.

A different approach is statistical and economic studies to determine price relations. The studies are of different kinds. One type uses regression analysis to try to explain time series of prices within a certain industry. Another type statistically determines the relevant demand and cost functions. Such studies are valuable and may contribute to a better understanding of how prices are formed. But this approach, too, has its limitations and must necessarily be supplemented by other methods.

Thus, although it is easy to recognize cost in the costing procedure, demand plays a nebulous role that is difficult to determine. The consequence is that the studies systematically underrate the role of demand compared with cost. In addition, there are numerous specific problems. The regression technique in itself is biased towards determining variable costs as proportional. The researcher is apt to use the accountant's concept of marginal cost, which is not the same as the economist's marginal cost. The studies invariably use the official list of prices. But in many cases, hardly anyone pays the official price; practically everybody obtains some form of discount.

The most direct method would be to determine the relevant concepts objectively. Thus, if price elasticity and marginal cost can be obtained for a given product, it can be determined directly whether the existing price is the optimum. This approach is only possible in exceptional cases, primarily because the price elasticity cannot be determined with sufficient exactness to permit analysis. The main obstacle is that the concepts can be interpreted in various ways. There is not one price elasticity; there are many. It depends on whether demand is considered in the short or long term, whether it is the actual demand curve or the one that the decision-maker believes exists, it depends on different assumptions as to competitor reactions, and so on.

Nor is marginal cost a clear concept. There may be a difference between marginal cost in the short and long-term. And managers may influence how marginal cost is to be interpreted. If they decide to keep the workforce stable in spite of variation in output, wages do not form part of marginal costs. If they choose to vary the number of workers, corresponding to variation in output, wages may constitute the main element of marginal cost. But how can an outsider know? Only in exceptional cases is it possible to determine price elasticity and marginal cost objectively.

Instead, a subjective approach could be tried. This can be done in two ways: from the outside or the inside. Normally outside researchers try to get insight into the pricing process. By interviewing the decision-makers

---

[7] A peculiar problem is that business executives may use the word theory in the opposite sense of the economists' use of the word.

researchers decide whether the actions of the decision-makers agree with the theory. For example, decision-makers may express an estimate of marginal cost and, furthermore, indicate that, in their opinion, demand is fairly inelastic. Based on this, researchers can then conclude that the current price is lower than the theoretically optimum price. But they will never be able to prove this point! A substantial part of research on pricing is subjective in the sense that researchers interpret the statements of the business decision-makers. And different researchers make different interpretations. Thus, some researchers used information on full costing to prove that there is disagreement between full cost and marginal theory. Others found it possible – based on the same information – to reconcile the seemingly conflicting theories.

What I have done is to adopt a subjective approach, but in the special variant in which it is seen mainly from the inside. I have not conducted any special research to obtain material for this book. It is based on the observations and impressions I have gathered over the years. In some companies, I have had continuous contact with the management over several years, thereby becoming familiar with their ways of thinking. Sometimes I have been asked for advice or a point of view without being directly involved in the setting of prices. I have formed my impressions of how the pricing process takes place and consistently drawn my own conclusions as to the relationship between theory and practice. I am fully aware that others may have different experiences and arrive at other conclusions.

Special interest is attached to situations in which I have been responsible for a price decision myself. It is only to be expected that I did my best to determine the optimum price so that the result would be a price in perfect harmony with the theory. I definitely have benefited from my theoretical knowledge and I believe that I have applied a theoretical line of reasoning. But that is not the same as saying that the optimum price was realized; or rather, that depends on how the optimum price is understood. Especially, there will be disagreement if it is interpreted in a short-term sense. There have been situations in which it was obvious that it would have paid off to select a higher price, at least in the short term, but probably also in the long term. In one situation my motivation was that I felt that a higher price would exploit the consumer.

I am fully aware of all the problems and uncertainties connected with a subjective approach. It may be difficult to see everything clearly when you are in the middle of it. But it is even more difficult for an outside observer to gain a correct impression of the main factors behind a specific decision.

As most of the examples in this book are based on my own experience, it follows that they originate from firms in Denmark. But the Danish cases are supplemented by other examples from the United States and western Europe. Over the years I have visited a number of firms and even acted as a consultant to a corporation in the United Kingdom. It is my impression that there is no difference between these countries when it comes to the principles of pricing. Other researchers have made the same observation: "It would seem from this brief review that the type and distribution of pricing practices within the countries reported largely replicate those of the United Kingdom."[8]

The text has been written under the assumption that the reader is familiar with the basic elements of neoclassical price theory. Thus, the elementary models are not presented.

I hope that the book will be of interest to students as a supplement to the traditional textbooks they have read. Elementary textbooks are based on assumptions so simplified that the gap between the real world and the theory is very wide. Students are sometimes so critical towards the theory that they reject it as a useless abstraction. They therefore need some guidance on how to apply the theory under more realistic assumptions, especially imperfect information, and they need to obtain an impression of the extent of the accordance between practical pricing and economic theory.

But I also hope that the text is of interest to other scholars. I believe that we should try to collect as much evidence as possible on how the pricing procedure looks in practice and use a variety of different methods. Many contributions have already been published. They have almost all been based on information obtained from companies, that is, by outside observers. This approach is useful and I have used it myself.

I also believe that it is valuable to relate the conclusions and observations of a professional economist, based on his active role in business decisions. It is of general interest for economic theory to have as many contributions as possible on the controversial subject of price theory and reality.

[8] Neil Dorward: *Pricing Decisions*, London, 1987, p. 117.

1. Normative and Descriptive Theories

1.1 The distinction between two types of theories

In principle, the two types of theory pursue different aims. However, they are interrelated and it is not always possible to make a clear distinction. The presentation in elementary textbooks is, in principle, a normative theory but is often supplemented by a number of illustrations from real life.

The purpose of a *normative* theory is to give guidance to the person who sets a price in practice.

The purpose of a *descriptive* theory is to explain how prices are actually determined in practice.

Whether a normative theory is useful depends on such factors as:

- Are the assumptions on which the theory is based the same as in practice? Or if that is not the case, can the theory be adjusted so that it can be applied to the conditions found in practice?

- Can the basic concepts of the theory be determined in practice, at least approximately?

- Is it fairly simple to apply the theory (as opposed to requiring complicated calculations and intricate reasoning)?

Although the value of a normative theory is fairly obvious, the purpose of a descriptive theory is not so clear.

A major purpose of any science is to explain phenomena observed in the real world. Therefore economic theory ought to be able to explain the formation of prices. This implies that it has to be able to answer such questions as:

- Why is the price for product A higher than for product B?

- Why is the price level for both A and B as it is?

- Why is a price stable over a certain period of time? And how can it suddenly change?

A descriptive theory has not only a value in itself. It can also be helpful to government, politicians and others by having a certain predictive value. Descriptive economic theory should be able to give sensible answers to such questions as:

- What is the likely effect on price of a tax imposed on a specific product?

- What will be the price effect of a specific increase in labor wages?

- If a general increase in demand occurs, what will be the effect on the prices of various articles?

In public debates, in newspaper articles and even in official statements, you will often find answers to questions like the ones above. In the majority of cases the argumentation is so primitive that you can hardly call it a theory; often it takes the form of postulates. A typical statement is that if costs are increased by a certain percentage, prices will increase by the same percentage.

There is a clear need for a more elaborate descriptive price theory that can give reliable answers to the questions above. However, no one theory will be able to describe and explain all types of pricing found in practice. To be acceptable, a descriptive theory must be able to give a fairly good explanation in the majority of cases, or at least give an approximate description within certain limits. For example, it may be applicable within certain trades but not others or be applicable in certain economies but not others.

1.2 Problems of a descriptive theory

The question of whether a theory conforms with pricing in practice is complicated. What is really meant by agreement between theory and practice?

The agreement may depend on *presentation*. Marginal theory is usually presented in textbooks by way of diagrams. However, nobody expects decision-makers to sit at their desks constructing marginal cost and revenue curves.

More important is whether there is harmony with respect to the way of *thinking*. To which extent do decision-makers think in marginal terms in practice? But it is possible to imagine a situation in which they think in marginal terms, but as a result of unrealistic assumptions, lack of knowledge or illogical thinking, arrive at a price that is not the optimum one?

It is therefore a special question of whether there is agreement in *result*. It is conceivable that the decision-makers end up with prices that are equal to the theoretical optimum prices, but their reasoning does not follow theory.

A further question is whether the agreement is *ex ante* or *ex post*. It is a hypothetical possibility that the moment the price is chosen for a new product, the demand curve changes. This could happen when, for example, customers, once quickly accustomed to a certain price, react against a price increase. It is possible that a statistical analysis would prove that the existing price fulfilled the condition that marginal revenue equalled marginal cost and therefore is in perfect agreement with the marginal theory. But it is a misleading observation, for the agreement is only *ex post*.

The goal of the firm may not be *profit* maximization. If that is the case, a descriptive theory should be able to explain how current prices reflect the firm's objectives.

Finally, it makes a difference whether the optimum price is considered in the short or long term.

To summarize, a descriptive theory may agree with pricing in practice as a result of the way price is presented, or is arrived at, or coincides unintentionally with theory, or shifts in time, or is congruent with company goals or whether it is viewed in a short- or long-term perspective.

1.3 Research problems

It is difficult for an outside researcher to judge whether a particular price agrees with a specific theory, for example, the marginal theory. The researcher will never be able to prove the motives and way of reasoning of the price-setters.

The researcher could simply ask the price-setters. However, many problems are connected with this method:

- The price setters are not always fully aware of their own motives and line of reasoning.

- They may be unable to express their motives.

- The researcher may not be able to understand the motives.

There are undoubtedly cases in which it is certain that a particular price is *not* in accordance with a specific theory, for example, the marginal theory. There are other situations in which it is highly likely that a price is in accordance. And then there are all the numerous cases in which there is some, but not perfect agreement.

Therefore, in the following presentation, many of the conclusions cannot be proved. They have a higher or lower degree of probability. Many statements have to be based on the observer's own impressions.

Scientific analysis involves not only observation but also measurement. It would be highly desirable if economic analysts could perform statistical surveys, which could give answers to such questions as:

- What percentage of firms apply a form of marginal reasoning?

- What percentage of firms use a formalized method of price calculation?

- What percentage of firms use some kind of full cost method?

  With such variables as:
  – different industries
  – different countries
  – different time periods
  – the size of the firm.

Such a procedure may be impossible. Making a grouping of practical cases into specific categories is problematic. The entire range, from perfectly correct marginal thinking with full information to examples of absolutely rigid full cost, would be apparent. It might be possible to make a statistical grouping of the formal procedures. However, the formal procedure does not always give a true picture of the actual pricing process.

As mentioned in the introduction, it is difficult for an outsider to get correct information. The use of mailed questionnaires is normally too primitive to tackle a problem as complicated as the pricing process. Personal interviews have a better chance of obtaining some insight.

1.4 A classification of theories

It might be convenient to place all different types of pricing into three broad categories:

– Category 1. This includes all the cases in which price is determined by factors on the *demand side* or at least so that demand considerations are dominant. No – or only negligible – regard is paid to costs.

The basis for the price-setter is such questions as: "What do such products usually cost?", "What price is the consumer likely to expect?", "What is the price of various substitutes to my product?" and "What price do I have to set in order to obtain a specific turnover?". In short, the price is determined by what the market will bear.

– Category 2. In this category are all the cases in which price is determined exclusively or mainly by *cost factors*. The major type is full cost pricing, which is based on an allocation of all costs to each individual product.

But also methods in which a predetermined percentage is added to variable unit costs fall in this category, because demand factors are not considered.

– Category 3. Prices are determined by the interplay between *demand* and *cost* factors. Prices set according to economic theory will be placed in this group.

In real life all cases cannot be placed in three clearly defined groups. At one extreme is rigid full cost in which no regard is paid to demand; at the other extreme price is solely determined by demand forces. But in between these two extremes is flexible full cost, in which some regard may be paid to demand factors, and market-determined prices, in which some regard is paid to cost factors.

It has already been said that a statistical classification into these three categories is meaningless. However, it might very well be that category 1 is the most common. Especially for small and medium-sized firms it is often felt that cost calculations are of limited value, when in reality it is the market that sets the price. Many examples can also be found in big firms in which a price is determined exclusively by market considerations.

In spite of this, the following pays most attention to the two other categories. For a normative theory, a purely market-determined pricing is of limited interest. It may be relevant if the goal is maximum turnover but not if it is profit maximization. The explanatory value for a descriptive theory is also limited. If a small competitor simply copies the prices of the leading firms, the interest is focused on how the big firms determine their prices.

One problem connected with market-determined prices requires comment: the chances that such prices correspond to the theoretically optimum prices.

In a great number of cases this is probably true. The firm may have no other choice than to sell at existing market prices – or to stop production. But definitely not always. Sometimes it is almost shocking to observe especially small and medium-sized firms simply set prices based on market factors with no regard to cost. Compared with economic theory, the firm may have specialized in the wrong products, and the price relations between the products may not be optimum. A small firm may, for example, copy the prices of a leading firm. But it might very well be that the cost structure is different in the two firms. It is even possible to find cases in which an analysis has demonstrated that a price is below variable costs.

It is unlikely that any general *descriptive* theory can explain all of the three categories. Correspondingly, you could imagine three different descriptive theories: a *market price* theory in harmony with category 1. A *full cost theory* that corresponds to category 2. And finally, a theory that takes both demand and cost factors into consideration; an example is the *marginal theory*. But the crucial problem is whether the marginal theory can also describe and explain a substantial part of the pricing process in categories 1 and 2.

We shall concentrate on whether marginal theory or full cost theory is most suitable as a general descriptive theory.

However, we are also interested in the usefulness of these conflicting theories as a *normative theory*. Even though it is obvious that there must be some connection between normative and descriptive theories, it has been found most practical to carry through the distinction between descriptive and normative theories. But with the implication that it is difficult to avoid some repetition.

2. Marginalism as a Normative Theory

2.1 The content of marginalism

Textbooks on price theory state that the optimum price of a given product can be determined by using three methods. The optimum price is determined when:

- The difference between *total* revenue and total cost is at its maximum.

- The *average* (gross or net) profit per unit multiplied by the number of units sold is highest.

- Marginal costs are equal to marginal revenue.

It is easy to demonstrate that when all three methods are correctly applied they will lead to the same result, as they all follow the same logic.

This presentation is based on simplified assumptions: the firm's goal is profit maximization, and all relevant concepts are known.

Even though these methods are expressions of the same basic logic, the marginal method is the favorite model of the theorists. In all presentations, emphasis is placed on this method to such an extent that modern price theory has become synonymous with marginalism, otherwise known as incremental reasoning. We shall follow this trend and concentrate on marginalism – even though the average and total methods could have been treated the same way.

Marginalism can be presented by the use of constructed numerical examples, by using mathematical equations or with the help of diagrams. The best known diagram is shown in Fig. 2.1, which is reproduced in all textbooks on price theory.

The intersection of the marginal cost and the marginal revenue curves determines the optimum volume, m_O, which in turn determines the optimum price, p_O.

The basic theory is then elaborated by varying the assumptions of market form, competitor reactions, multiple products, interdependence of products and whether it is in the long or short term. The theory can be extended to cover any problem, on the condition that the underlying assumptions can be stated explicitly. For all models the central point remains the same: that the optimum price is when marginal cost is equal to marginal revenue.

In principle, a marginal theory is formulated as a normative theory because it states the conditions to be fulfilled in order that a price can be

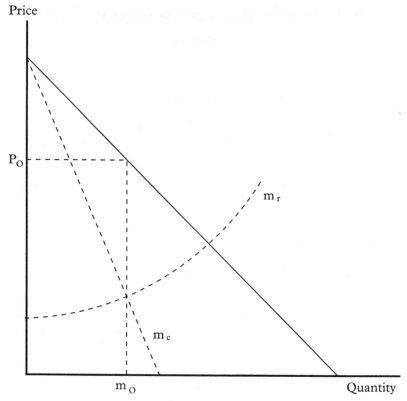

Figure 2.1

in optimum. In its most simplified form, the assumptions are: a one-product firm, no competitors, perfect information and profit maximization in the short term.

These elementary conditions are rarely fulfilled in practice, and the theory is therefore expanded with more complicated assumptions. These could include multiple products with known costs, demand relations between the different products and various assumptions about competitor reactions.

A dilemma of normative theories is that, if the theory is to be relevant and reliable, it can be so general that its usefulness is limited.

To be used in practical application, a normative theory needs to be easy to understand and simple to apply. The theory may be formulated in a simplified form, with the advantage that it is fairly clear and leads to specific results. This could lead to the risk that the conditions for its applicability are not fulfilled – and the results are therefore misleading.

If the theory is elaborated to include all relevant factors, it becomes adequate and relevant, but with the consequence that the models become so complicated and vague that they hardly lead to any result at all.

Let us focus on the theory in the simplified form, in which only one product is taken into consideration and perfect information and short-term profit maximization are assumed.

The problem is whether such a model gives meaningful guidance.

In a constructed numerical example in which all relevant facts are known, a correct use of the theory will invariably lead to the optimum solution. But is the model useful in practice?

In principle, the model requires that the demand function be known. In textbooks the demand curve is usually drawn as a straight line. But all analyses and all experiences show that demand curves are never linear. This is not decisive for an elementary theory, in which the central point is that the demand curve slopes downward – and for illustration it might just as well be drawn as a straight line.[9] But the consequence is that the price elasticity varies from (minus) infinity to zero, which is absolutely unrealistic. To apply the theory it is (normally) irrelevant to know the entire demand curve. What is relevant is to be able to make a fair estimate of price elasticity at the current production level. And an assumption of a constant price elasticity is more realistic than an assumption of a straight demand curve. Especially for a new product you will hardly ever have any idea of the entire demand curve – but you may have a workable idea of price elasticity.

Managers will generally have some, but imperfect knowledge of relevant price elasticities, and seldom will they be able to give numerical values to the elasticities. But in numerous cases their knowledge may be sufficient for an application of the theory.

But the difficulties are great. The first one is that their knowledge often will be relative, in the sense that they are convinced that product A is more elastic than product B. They draw the conclusion that product B can carry a higher contribution margin than A, but they feel that the marginal theory gives them insufficient guidance as to the absolute price level.

Should it be 2, 5 or 20 times the marginal cost?

The second difficulty is that the elementary theory makes the assumption that, at a given moment, there is one and only one demand curve. But often this is an unrealistic assumption. It is well known that there may be a difference between the demand function in the short and the long term.[10] But even in the short term, various factors may have an influence. Let us use an actual case as illustration. In 1973 the Danish

---

[9] This is clearly brought out by F. Machlup: "The wide range they cover was clearly designed to enable those in the back rows of the class room to make out what goes on the blackboard." F. Machlup: "Marginal analysis and empirical research", *American Economic Review*, 1946, p. 522.

[10] Of course the demand function is also influenced by advertising and other sales efforts.

Government introduced a 50% subsidy on iron preparations. If the selling price was doubled, the net price the consumer would have to pay would remain unchanged – and according to the original demand curve, the quantity sold should remain the same. But everybody would expect that a drastic price increase would be met by a violent reaction by the consumers, who would find such a policy abusive. Thus, the demand curve itself has changed as a result of the subsidy. (The actual price reactions of the producers will be discussed in chapter 6.)

The third difficulty is also well known, i.e., that the demand curve depends on the reaction of the competitors. Usually a demand curve is defined under the condition of no competitor reaction, but with the obvious consequence that, if a decision is based on this demand curve and the competitors actually do react, the outcome is not the optimum one. Thus, a condition for marginal reasoning to be acceptable is that it be based on the interpretation of the demand curve that is the relevant one. If this condition is not fulfilled, the result of marginal reasoning may easily become misleading.

A fourth difficulty is that the elementary theory is based on the assumption of a free and unregulated market. But in our days this condition will not be fulfilled in many cases. In the example with iron preparations, it is likely that consumers will react to a drastic price increase, but it is almost certain that the government will intervene and force the prices down. Thus, for the relevant demand curve, government reactions also have to be taken into consideration.

But even for a firm that enjoys a monopoly position, an application of marginal reasoning may give catastrophic results.

Let us use two examples as illustrations of how even a sophisticated use of marginal reasoning may give erroneous results. The first example is a Danish newspaper which enjoys a monopoly position, as it is the only daily within its region. The head of the marketing department is not only familiar with modern price theory but also deliberately attempts to apply the theory in practice. Much energy has been used in analyzing the relevant markets. By using multiple regression techniques, the marketing manager has tried to gain insight into the relevant demand functions and has obtained a fair idea of the price elasticities.

One of the "products" studied was "House for sale" advertisements. The analysis indicated a relatively inelastic demand. This conformed with the marketing manager's line of reasoning: it would be unthinkable to have a house for sale in the region without an advertisement in the only local newspaper. Furthermore, real estate brokers can normally pass the cost of advertising on to the owner of the house. Thus, everything convinced this manager that the demand curve was as indicated by A_1A_1 in the figure. The logical consequence was that the current price, p_0, was below the optimum level and therefore could be safely increased to p_1. This was done.

What was the result?

Two of the real estate brokers found the price increase abusive and an

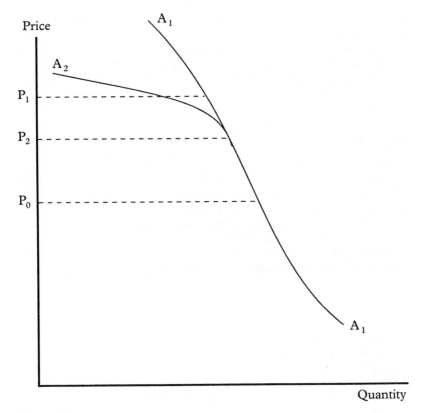

Figure 2.2

unfair exploitation of a monopoly position. So they took the initiative to organize other brokers and began distributing – weekly trade paper advertising houses for sale. From one week to the next, the volume of real estate advertising in the original daily newspaper fell dramatically. Thus, the demand curve turned out to be A_2A_1 and not A_1A_1 as anticipated. The optimum price was not p_1, but p_2.

Could the marketing manager have known this beforehand?

Of course the manager could have reasoned that the higher the price was raised, the greater the risk that some form of substitution would come to market. However, the manager could not have known in advance that a broker would take an initiative. If no one had reacted, p_1 would have been the optimum price. The lesson learned in this instance was that a logical application of the marginal method may lead to disaster when the basic assumptions are not fulfilled.

The second example is illustrative for the reason that a trained theoretical economist was asked to determine the optimum price before a new product was brought on the market.

In institutions such as hospitals the requirements for cleanliness are extremely high. Traditionally the process of cleaning has been done by use of soap, water and hard work.

A few years ago, a firm in Denmark introduced a new and efficient product specifically made for this type of cleaning. Extensive experiments proved the value of the new product through great savings in labor costs, so the firm had confidence in the market potential. A price had to be set.

The theoretical economist, who was asked to determine the likely optimum price, started by assuming that, when the product was brought on the market, potential users would calculate whether it would give savings large enough to justify using the product. He made these calculations himself in order to determine the equilibrium price at which the old and the new alternative had the same value. The result constituted the maximum price, and in order to have a margin of safety, the theoretical optimum price would probably be somewhat lower.

Through systematic experiments he could calculate the number of labor hours saved for different types of use. With a knowledge of labor costs, it was possible to construct a demand curve, based on the as-

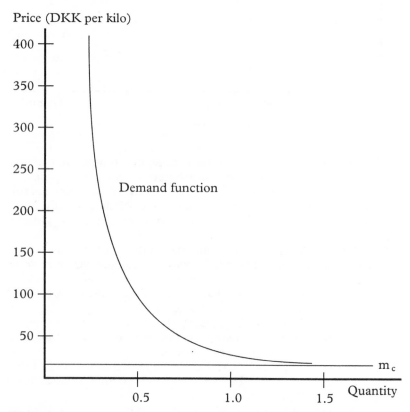

Price (DKK per kilo)

Demand function

m_c

Quantity

0.5   1.0   1.5

Figure 2.3

sumption that all potential users would make rational calculations to the extent that it was economical to substitute the new product for their current brand. The result is illustrated in Fig. 2.3.

There was no problem estimating marginal costs. A great deal of time had been spent in developing the new product, but the manufacturing process was a simple process of mixing.

With fair estimates of demand and marginal costs, the theoretical maximum price was calculated as DKK 760 per kilogram. In order to have a safety margin, the optimum price was thought somewhat less. Thus, we have a perfectly clear application of marginal theory.

The product was actually introduced at a price of DKK 14 per kilo! Evidently theory and practice give widely different results.

How was the price of DKK 14 chosen?

It was not chosen according to any sophisticated full cost calculation, market research or the like. It was chosen using vague criteria such as "What do such types of cleaning products usually cost?" and "What price level is the customer likely to expect?". Another factor was so evident that it was, more or less consciously, taken into consideration. As the production process was fairly simple, it was foreseen that, within a maximum of six months, a competing product would be brought to the market.[11] The resulting subsequent drastic price reduction would be harmful to the image of the firm.

Can the price be characterized as an example of entry-deterrent pricing?

The answer is negative, even though the risk of potential competition played a role, but even a somewhat higher price would still have deterred entrants. Actually it was a mixture of many different considerations.

Also, in this case an application of a simplified marginal theory would have led to a catastrophe, as the basic assumptions were unrealistic.

For marginal reasoning, the relevant cost concept is marginal cost. Once more: in a constructed numerical example with a clear distinction between fixed and variable costs, it is no problem to give the concept marginal cost a clear content.

But is the concept useful in practice?

The separation of costs into a fixed and a variable part is highly useful in an elementary textbook and is of considerable pedagogical value. But as soon as you are beyond the beginning stage, the distinction should be abandoned. In numerous practical situations the separation is too diffuse to be useful.

With the exception of materials and piece-rate payments, all factors of production have a certain capacity – and their costs are actually semi-variable. Each time a capacity limit is reached, a cost increase will occur.

---

[11] The firm contemplated taking out a patent, but refrained from doing so because it would delay the product introduction.

Let us imagine a firm in the electrochemical industry that is contemplating widening its range of products with a new product. As a basis for its decision, the management wants to determine the marginal costs of this new product.

Management may take the point of view that marginal costs include the cost of materials only, because at present there is a certain labor reserve. They may realize that this is only temporary. Over time a gradual increase in the labor force is expected as a consequence of a general increase in production. Thus, labor should be regarded as a variable and not fixed cost. For example, one of the current supervisors can supervise the new production, but if the product becomes a success, it will sooner or later be necessary to hire one more. Likewise, there is at present space for the new product in the trucks, but eventually a new truck will have to be bought. Thus, the new product will have to cover its share of transportation costs. In a similar way, the number of administrative staff would have to be increased. Rent is initially unaffected, but the addition of the new product may lead to the acquisition of extra space.

Short-term marginal cost is a fairly clear concept. But long-term marginal cost is not. The long-term marginal cost of the new product must be defined as the difference between the total of all future costs, when the new product is included, and what the total sum of all future costs will be if the new product is not included. Managers may take the attitude that this concept is too theoretical to be applicable in practice. They want to know how to determine the long-term marginal costs.

This cannot be done in any exact, logical way. The managers may try to estimate how the existence of the new product may influence different costs in the future. Or they may try to use a system in which part of other costs are allocated to the new product. But no matter what criteria for allocation are chosen, a certain degree of arbitrariness is involved. If the method is carried to its extreme, a part of all costs are allocated to the new product, which is equivalent to a full cost calculation. Thus, in reality, we end in a method of full costing.

Managers may choose to base their decisions on short-term marginal cost, with the obvious risk of making the wrong decision. Again and again, the mistake is made in practice that the increase in total costs caused by the adoption of a new product is underestimated. Or managers base the considerations on a calculation of full cost as an approximation to long-term marginal cost, but with the risk of overestimating the cost increases, and refuse to adopt a new product – even though it might have turned out to become remunerative.

2.2 Presentation of the theory

One objection to the marginal theory in the form in which it usually is presented in textbooks is that it is not adjusted to the manager's way of thinking. They do not sit and construct demand and cost curves. This objection, however, does not carry much weight. It is not decisive whether the theory is presented one way or the other.

A typical approach in practice is to use a form of mark-up pricing. For example, the procedure may be to determine the price by adding a percentage mark-up to direct or variable unit costs.

The marginal method can be adjusted to this line of reasoning. This is sometimes demonstrated in textbooks.[12] A presentation in this form may be useful for a manager, as it is more in accordance with practical thinking.

On the condition that variable costs are proportional, it is easy to demonstrate that marginal reasoning can be adjusted to a mark up procedure.

The basic criteria for a price being optimum is that:

$$price = MC[e/(e - 1)]$$

As MC = AVC (average variable cost), this can be reformulated as

$$price = AC + [-1/(e + 1)]AVC$$

Let us assume that e = -5: we will then have

$$price = AVC + [-1/(-5 + 1)]AVC$$

or

$$price = AVC + 25\% \text{ of AVC.}$$

Thus, if the price elasticity is estimated to be 5, you add a mark-up of 25%.

In general, this can be formulated as:

Numerical price elasticity	Mark-up in percent
2	100.0
3	50.0
4	33.3
5	25.0
6	20.0
10	11.1
50	2.0

Presented in this way, marginal theory does not require knowledge of the entire demand curve but only of price elasticity. This is in accord-

---

[12] An example is Evan J. Douglas, *Managerial Economics: Theory, Practice and Problems*, Englewood Cliffs, NJ: Prentice-Hall, 1983.

ance with the way business executives are thinking, and the formula can be immediately useful when conditions are not too complicated. This may be the case within retailing, in handicraft or in a small industrial plant, in which it is defensible to make a clear separation between fixed and variable costs. Within retailing, the purchase price may be considered equivalent to variable costs. The table above tells retailers that a percentage mark-up should be based on an estimate of a product's price elasticity. This may be a variation on what they have always done: "We charge what the market will bear; apparently that is what you call price elasticity."

Thus, under simplified assumptions, the marginal theory may be applied in practice. But often conditions in practice require that the assumptions become more complicated. Then either the result will not be correct, or the theory must be modified. Thus, within retailing, other costs than purchase price may be relevant for the marginal cost of each product or product group. For example:

- Some products such as vegetables require a certain amount of handling.

- There is waste connected with some products but not others.

- The rate of turnover varies for different groups of products. Milk, on average, will be in stock for a few days, whereas some household appliances may stay in the store for several months.

- Some product groups require special installations, such as a deep-freezer for frozen meat and fish.

The fundamental theory may be adjusted in such a way that the marginal approach can still be used. The retailer will have to estimate – or analyze – how much waste is connected with different products and adjust the marginal cost correspondingly. The essential point is whether there is a relevant causal relationship. This will be the case for waste, but it is doubtful for the deep-freezer. The cost of the deep-freezer is clearly caused by the frozen goods, but it might be regarded as a fixed cost, which is not relevant for marginal costs.

The more complicated the assumptions become, the greater the risk that the simplified theory will give misleading results. Therefore, the theory has to be expanded and adjusted to handle more complicated problems.

Normally it will be possible to calculate short-term marginal cost. But if management is not satisfied with a short-term approach, how can it obtain an estimate of long-term marginal costs? As already mentioned, such an estimate may be obtained in different ways. One way is to make a *technical* approach. For example, for a new product to be introduced you estimate the physical need of the various factors of production, the prices of these and how the introduction of the new product will influence the production process of existing products.

Another approach is the *cost accounting* method, in which the necessary information is obtained from the cost accounting system. This will imply that part of the overhead is allocated to the new product. The technical method will refer to the present or the future, whereas cost accounting, in principle, refers to the past. But in principle, it is possible to use past data as a basis to estimate future costs.

It is not possible here to describe all the imaginable cost accounting systems actually used. Nor is it possible to discuss all the different problems connected with cost accounting. The existing literature on the principles of cost accounting is already overwhelming and, in certain aspects, controversial. Various authors have different views on the advantages and drawbacks of different methods. We have to confine ourselves to the basic principles and omit all detailed refinements, no matter how interesting they may be.

Our fundamental problem is: will existing systems of cost accounting be able to give management the information necessary to estimate (different interpretations of) marginal costs? As we are only interested in the basic principles, we shall limit ourselves to two alternative systems of cost allocation.

2.3 Relevant cost information

The first method we will discuss is widely used all over the world. Overhead is calculated as a certain percentage of (some form of) variable costs. This may be labor costs only or labor plus material costs. The system is found in a great number of variations. For example, some types of overhead but not all are allocated to the individual products. All these variations are of minor importance. The basic issue is that you use a relatively simple method in which all types of overhead are allocated to each product.

The basic information management receives can be regarded as an estimate of the total average unit cost. Normally management will not only receive this figure but will have the entire calculation, so that it can break up the unit cost into its components.

Whether a system in which all types of overhead are allocated as a percentage of variable costs can be brought in harmony with the marginal theory depends on the circumstances. In a great number of cases the information is definitely misleading. If overhead is a fixed cost – also in the long term – it is artificially made variable by calculating it as a percentage of variable costs. The other extreme is that overhead in the long term actually behaves as variable costs. This may happen in a progressive and rapidly developing firm. I have personally experienced a case in which it was defensible to interpret the costs calculated as a percentage of variable costs as an approximation to long-term marginal costs. The explanation was that the company found itself in a period of rapid development, so rapid that a doubling of production not only required more workers, but also an equivalent increase in the administrative staff, in buildings and so on. Thus, it was a fair estimate that an increase in production of a particular product over time causes an equivalent increase in overhead. But this case is an exception. The other extreme is more common, i.e., that the overhead must be regarded as fixed costs – even in the long term. Any allocation will be directly misleading. And then you have all the cases in between, in which there may be some effect on overhead. The phenomena of "creeping indirect costs" can often be observed. Thus, if you base your decisions on variable costs alone, you are apt to make a mistake. And if you instead base it on calculated full cost, you make another mistake. As a rule, the information is not sufficient for a decision on whether a specific product should be dropped. The pertinent information is the level of cost savings achieved if the product is dropped, and the calculation does not tell that directly.

Neither does the calculation give the relevant information for pricing decisions. The calculation only gives the unit costs at a particular level of production. But what is relevant is how costs will be affected by variation in the level of production.

Carried to its extreme, the method is really a sort of full cost calculation. We shall revert to this method and discuss its merits and drawbacks in chapter 5.

For a modern multi-product company, the above method is too primitive to give sufficient guidance for management decisions. To obtain the information that permits marginal reasoning, the firm needs a more refined system of cost accounting that is able to give management the relevant information. In principle, the system may be constructed so that it gives data for (long-term) marginal costs directly, or it may be that a fair estimate of these costs can be deduced from the cost data.

Many contributions have been published by economists, and a number of systems have been constructed and discussed. For some years the most advanced debate was found in the German literature.[13] As this debate attracted little attention outside Germany, it is appropriate to base the following presentation on the literature in English. A useful starting-point could be Kaplan's thoughts, which have created a lively debate.[14] The method proposed by Kaplan and others is called activity-based costing or the ABC method. In the ABC method, overhead (including costs normally regarded as fixed) is allocated to individual products. The underlying idea is that there is a causal relationship between the

---

[13] For example: G. Lassmann, *Die Produktionsfunktion und ihre Bedeutung für die Betriebwirtschaftliche Kostentheorie*, Köln, 1958.

[14] R.S. Kaplan, "Measuring manufacturing performance: a new challenge for managerial accounting research", *The Accounting Review*, 1983; R.S. Kaplan, "The evolution of management accounting", *The Accounting Review*, 1984; R. Cooper & R.S. Kaplan, "How cost accounting distorts product costs", *Management accounting*, 1988; R. Cooper & R.S. Kaplan, "Measure costs right: make the right decisions", *Harvard Business Review*, 1988.

end product and the resources used to manufacture it. A product may benefit from machine capacity, research activities and marketing campaigns and is therefore charged for using these resources. No single allocation criterion is used, and each type of cost is allocated to the products that generated it.

Let us illustrate the working of the system by comparing two products. Product A is manufactured mainly by hand and product B is produced in a highly automated fashion. Obviously, overhead allocation as a percentage of labor costs will give a distorted result. Under the ABC method, B benefits from factory overhead and is charged accordingly.

The basic idea is that each product should be charged for the costs it generates. Therefore, a product that is advertised heavily or requires extensive service will be charged more than other products. Likewise, set-up costs or start-up costs are allocated according to the number of production runs for each product. Naturally, such a system raises a huge number of problems. Research and development costs should be traced to the products that benefited from the outlays. It is obvious that some costs cannot be allocated in a meaningful way, such as costs connected with research, which has been in vain in the sense that it never materializes in marketable products. Costs for which no causal relationship can be established are not assigned to a product rather than being allocated arbitrarily. Evidently such a system requires sophisticated methods of cost allocation, but modern computer techniques make this possible.

2.4 Cost information for optimum pricing

In a modern multi-product industrial company, the marginal theory in its rudimentary form is not sufficient for management decisions. The theory has to be expanded to tackle the complicated problems in such an enterprise. This requires management to have at its disposal relevant information on costs. If management has the benefit of an ABC system, will it be possible to adjust incremental reasoning in such a way that optimum decisions can be achieved?

The two pertinent questions are: will it be possible with the aid of an ABC system to determine whether a product line should be discontinued? And is it possible to determine optimum prices by using this system logically?

Let us as illustration use an example adapted from Kaplan and Cooper. A company manufacturing ballpoint pens has an annual output of two million pens. Exactly half of these are blue pens, which are produced in a continuous process. The remaining million are produced in assorted colors according to demand. Thus, 10,000 lavender pens are manufactured a year. Which consequences does this difference have for whether a product should be dropped, and what consequences will it have for the pricing of particular products? The production process for the lavender pen is not continuous, but is divided up into separate runs. Let us assume that the production series is set up 10 times a year, each time manufacturing a total of 1,000 units. Labor and material costs are the same for the blue and the lavender pen.

From a short-term point of view, both pens are remunerative if a price is obtained that is higher than labor plus material costs. But also the price should be the same, because marginal costs are equivalent – on the condition that there is no difference in price elasticities.

But are the long-term optimum prices also the same?[15] If management wants to determine the long-term optimum price, it has to base its considerations on long-term marginal costs. But what are the long-term marginal costs of the two products? Let us assume that the company uses an ABC system that not only informs about the unit costs of each product but separates the cost calculation into various parts: labor, materials, allocated capacity costs, allocated development costs, and so on. The special set-up costs are clearly caused by the lavender pen. Is that relevant for marginal cost and thus for pricing? That depends. If a price increase results in the production of only 8,000 units a year, this may imply that set-up costs are only incurred 8 times rather than 10 times a year. This information is relevant for pricing. However, if there are still 10 production runs a year, each producing only 800 units, there will be no set-up cost savings. Under these conditions, set-up costs do not form part of marginal costs and are irrelevant for pricing.

According to the system, the costs that can be said to be caused by the lavender pen should be allocated to that product. But some of these costs, such as development costs, may belong to the past and thus be irrelevant for estimating marginal costs. And as to allocated overhead, the real problem is whether a change in the production of the lavender pen may have any influence on overhead. The ABC system does not give this information directly, but it may form a better point of departure for an estimate than the more primitive systems.

The short-term marginal costs are the same for the blue and the lavender pen. But what about long-term marginal costs? That depends. If a cut in the production of the lavender pen has the consequence that annual set-up costs are lowered, and the savings in overhead are relatively higher than for the blue pen, then the marginal cost is higher for the lavender than the blue pen. And this may lead to charging a higher price for the lavender pen. But a special analysis is necessary to clarify this.

In an ABC system, the unit costs of low-volume products become higher. This may lead management to charge a higher price for the lavender pen than for the standard blue pen. But that is not necessarily

---

[15] The distinction between optimum in the short term and the long term is often confusing for students. They sometimes believe that the short-term price is the one you set now, while the long-term price will have to be set some time in the future. It should be emphasized that both prices are set now. The difference consists of how long a time horizon you take into consideration.

a logical consequence, for (short-term as well as long-term) marginal costs may be the same for both articles. The paradox is that it might be a correct decision to charge a higher price for the lavender pen – but based on demand and not cost. There are good reasons to suppose that customers who strongly desire a lavender pen will also be willing to pay more than for a blue pen. Furthermore, if the price were the same, fewer manufacturers would manufacture the lavender pen, thereby reducing competition and make a higher price possible. But this result is more accidental than logical. The theoretically correct method must still be to estimate marginal costs as correctly as possible and then set the final price according to elasticity considerations.

The other problem was how to determine whether or not a product or product line should be maintained – not only in the short term but also the long term. An ABC system calculates the unit cost of a product as the direct variable costs plus the indirect costs that are considered to be caused by that particular product. Let us assume that the calculated unit cost of the lavender pen is higher than the current price. Does that imply that the company is losing money on the product and it should be dropped?

Not necessarily. The problem is the traditional one that historical accounting is reporting on the past, but management decisions are for the future. The direct variable costs will cease if the pen is dropped. The set-up costs will disappear if the production of the lavender pen is discontinued – and this is relevant. Other allocated costs may or may not be saved. Research costs, even though caused by that pen, will not be saved. An advanced ABC system enables a separation into costs that are affected and those that are not, but it does not automatically give that information.

And it must still be remembered that due regard must be taken to considerations on the demand side: the advantage of carrying a full assortment, direct substitution and complementary effects, competitive considerations and so on.

2.5 Implications for practice

The fundamental question is whether the marginal theory is useful as a normative theory. Often management will find that the theory offers insufficient help. In many modern industrial plants, marginal costs only constitute a small fraction of total costs, and it is not uncommon that marginal costs constitute only 5% or 10% of total costs. Managers feel that they cannot determine a price on basis of 5% of the costs and a vague feeling of what the price elasticity is.

In the elementary theory, cost is conceived as a function of the volume of production. But today it is often the number of product variations and product differences that is costly. When the production run of a specific number has started up, the production process goes more or less automatically.

Thus, the elementary theory is not always applicable. But of course there are many situations in which even the most simplified theory may be helpful. The theory certainly has its advantages. It is logical, easy to understand and leads to a clear result. But if the simplistic assumptions are not fulfilled, it will give misleading results. The alternative is to expand the theory by making more realistic but also more complicated assumptions.

The basis theory assumes that, in a given situation, there is one and only one demand curve. But as already emphasized, at a given time there may be a number of demand curves, each defined under specific assumptions. A newspaper may be fully aware that there is one demand curve for real estate advertising under the assumption that real estate brokers will not react and another if they do. The newspaper cannot know beforehand which assumption is realistic. Furthermore, there may be differences between short- and long-term demand curves, demand curves under autonomous or conjectural behavior and with or without government interference. There is not one optimum price. There are many. How can you make use of the marginal theory under such circumstances?

In principle, it is perfectly possible to extend the theory and elaborate models under more complicated assumptions. Instead of having one demand curve, you can operate with many and with an estimate of the probability of each. You can calculate a number of alternatives in order to determine which is the best one. In principle, you can always use the marginal way of reasoning, when you either have perfect information or are able to attach probabilities to the different alternatives. The problem is not to establish the relevant theory and construct the appropriate models. The problem is how useful such models are in practice.

On the cost side, you have to give up the primitive distinction between variable and fixed costs. A necessity for the models to be correct is that you have a much more detailed knowledge of the cost structure. Costs are a multidimensional function of a number of factors, and you have to obtain knowledge of the relevant parts of this function. For example, you will have to know that, under certain conditions, the capacity of a factor of production is sufficient, and under other conditions capacity has to be increased. In one situation workers may be willing to work overtime; in another situation they will refuse.[16] Again, if you have per-

---

[16] An example from my own experience. In a textile plant, the management accepted an extra (and big) order even though existing capacity was fully utilized. The work had to be done on overtime. Management had special reasons to accept the order despite the expectation that the agreed price would not cover the extra cost. Variable costs were supposed to be progressive for two reasons: the (female) workers would be tired and productivity lower plus overtime pay. It turned out that costs were degressive, because the workers increased their productivity in order not to come home too late. The result was that the extra order was highly remunerative. But how could management know? Nobody would expect that the same could happen again within the same plant.

fect information on all cost relations, there is no problem in using the marginal approach.

You can expand and adjust the theory to be logically correct under more and more complicated conditions. More and more factors might be included, making the model more realistic. This carries the commensurate risk that it becomes so complicated that it is hardly useful. The words marginal theory are simply the label on a box, including everything. The theory ends up with the diffuse recommendation that you should take everything into consideration and find the best possible result.

The theorist may be interested in constructing more and more sophisticated models, in which you try to incorporate as many relevant factors as possible. The application of such models will require access to computer services. Such models have been constructed and used successfully. And still more will be constructed in the future. Nevertheless, they are only of limited interest. The average business executive is still mostly interested in simple methods that are easy to apply. They do not necessarily have to lead to the optimum. What practice needs is a method that gives approximate but acceptable results.

Most businesses offer a range of products. In extreme cases a firm may have to set as many as 100 prices a day, which makes it virtually impossible each time to estimate marginal cost and marginal revenue. The pricing process will often be routine. And the theory has to be adjusted to these conditions. This can be done by establishing general guidelines. In the retail business, for example, on one group of products a gross margin of 20% is added to the purchase price, on another 30% and so on. The obvious risk is that, under special circumstances, a price may be absurd. Under more complicated conditions, such as an industrial plant with thousands of products, a system of routine will have to include some method of cost allocation. Such a method will hardly lead to optimum prices but to prices that might be accepted. The question is whether such methods still can be characterized as marginal thinking.

The normative theory is often understood as normative in the sense that, when the optimum solution is determined, this solution "ought" to be carried out in practice. Of course this does happen. In general, the result of marginal reasoning is not "binding" in itself, but its value consists in supplying decision-makers with the information based on which they can make decisions. The optimum is found under the assumption of profit maximization. But there may be various reasons for deviating from that.

Let me use an example as illustration of the value of the normative theory. The management of the Tivoli amusement park in Copenhagen wanted to have the optimum price for a ride in the roller coaster determined. The cost structure offered no difficulties. The problem lay in estimating the demand curve. By systematic price experiments over a whole season, a perfect (curve-linear) demand curve could be constructed.[17] This was an example in which it was possible to draw demand and cost curves and determine the optimum price exactly as in the textbooks. The theoretical optimum price was higher than the current price. In spite of this, management did not immediately raise the price. But in addition, the analysis clearly demonstrated that different types of price discrimination would be rational. You did not even need an analysis to realize this. The fact that, in certain periods, people were standing in line is a clear indication that prices could be increased. A consequent marginal reasoning indicated that it would pay A) to have higher prices Saturday and Sunday nights, B) lower prices on weekday afternoons, C) lower prices on rainy days, D) that by paying a premium price you could get ahead of the waiting line.

The only proposal that was carried through was alternative B. Management could base its decisions on as perfect information as possible. But it took other factors than profit maximization into consideration. It was fully aware of that some forms of price discrimination did not correspond to the image of the park. But management has the knowledge that, if some time in the future an increase in income is necessary, it knows how to obtain it.

This example illustrates that marginal theory may be useful, even though the goal is not profit maximization.

But our main interest is attached to the problem of whether marginal reasoning can lead to the price that maximizes profit.

We have already stated that most acts of price-setting have to follow a pattern of routine, such as when hundreds of prices have to determined every day. It does not make sense in each case to try to determine marginal revenue and cost. You have to follow more or less standardized decision rules, which often take the form of rules of thumb. In a later chapter we shall evaluate some of the rules commonly found in practice.

But our central interest is attached to the situations in which it is very important to arrive at the right decision in regard to price. This will not only be the case when a new product is introduced on the market but also when a competitor's challenge is dangerous and when a drastic price change is contemplated.

It is easy in practice to find catastrophic blunders; it is a little more

---

[17] The experiment was carried out so that prices were varied in a predetermined way, taking due regard to such factors as time of the year, weekdays or weekends. The price was never advertised, only indicated at the ticket booths. Management had set up the condition that if any newspaper began to wonder about the seemingly senseless variations in price, the experiment had to be discontinued. But nobody seemed to notice what was going on. Naturally the number of tickets sold was registered, but in addition the number of people standing in line was systematically counted.

Based on these observations, a perfect demand curve could be constructed. The result was surprising to everybody, including management, who had believed that demand was relatively inelastic. Actually the demand was highly price-sensitive. With the highest prices of the experiment there was never a line; with the lowest there were occasions where it lasted more than one hour from the moment you took your place in the line until you got a ride!

difficult to find sophisticated and perfect decisions on price. But they do exist.

It is characteristic for such cases that management uses a systematic approach and applies modern techniques of analysis and pricing methods. The market is thoroughly analyzed by such techniques as personal interviews, conjoint measurement, regression analysis and so on. Simultaneously, cost is analyzed, not as a traditional primitive cost calculation but as an analysis of how different factors may influence costs. It also has to be realized which outside factors may influence the result. All these factors are added together into a systematic scheme for price decisions. Of course you have no guarantee that you will end up with the optimum decision – there will always exist a factor of uncertainty. But you may have better chances than with more primitive methods. The problem is whether such elaborate methods can be listed under the heading of marginal theory. At least the approach is a far cry from the price models of economic textbooks.

In a situation in which it is very important for management to make a right decision as to price, still more factors have to be taken into consideration. We treat price isolated, but that is an oversimplification, as advertising, quality, service and so on may also influence the optimum decision. Even though these factors are important, we shall disregard them in the following.

But there is one more factor from which we cannot abstract: the existence of competitors. In a systematic pricing program, it is necessary to analyze not only the customers but also the competitors. It may be more difficult to predict the behavior of competitors than of customers.

But there are many examples in which this has been done with success. A study of past behavior may give some clues as to future reactions. And even such a simple device as an enumeration of the alternatives open to competitors may be helpful.

At this moment we shall not proceed with the problems connected with competition but postpone a more systematic discussion to chapter 6. But still, the degree of competition is so important for the relevance of various price models that in the illustrations we bring in the next chapters it may in some cases be relevant to describe the competitive situation.

3. Marginalism as a Descriptive Theory

3.1 Statement of the problem

The purpose of a normative theory is to give support to the decision-maker in practice, whereas a descriptive theory is for the benefit of outsiders. For economic theory, it is a purpose in itself to be able to describe and explain the pricing process. But as previously mentioned, public authorities may also be interested in the predictive value of the theory. If a government contemplates taxing a certain commodity, it is a relevant question as to which effect such a tax is likely to have on consumer prices.

The fundamental problems with descriptive theories have already been mentioned in chapter 1. It is unrealistic to expect any theory to give an exhaustive description and explanation of all forms of pricing found in practice. We must be satisfied if a theory can give a description of for example general tendencies, some interesting phenomena or the pricing of some important products. But it is also essential that the theory have a certain predictive value.

In the elementary textbooks, the marginal theory is, in principle, formulated as a normative theory. It stipulates the correct way of reasoning to find the optimum solution. Does it also have relevance as a descriptive theory? This question is sometimes formulated: is there agreement between theory and practice? As already mentioned in chapter 1, this question has to be stated much more precisely if it is to be answered meaningfully.

The difficulties are great. The first complication is that the theory normally is based on an assumption of profit maximization, usually in the short term. Whether the theory is adequate as a descriptive theory may depend on whether the assumption of profit maximization is realistic or not. Thus, if the presentation in the textbooks is based on short-term profit maximization, whereas practice focuses on the long term, there will be no agreement between theory and practice.

In principle, the marginal method can be extended to achieve any type of goal, on the condition that this goal can be stated precisely. For example, the goal may be maximum turnover with profit restrictions. For a normative theory you can assume that the decision-makers are aware of their goal. But for a descriptive theory the relevant question is how outsiders can have any knowledge of what the goal is.

The second complication has already been mentioned in chapter 2. Marginal cost and marginal income are elusive concepts that can be interpreted in different ways. From a short-term point of view the concepts are relatively clear, but when you extend your reasoning to the long term, there is hardly any limit to how they can be interpreted. Therefore, when we discuss the adequacy of marginal reasoning as a descriptive theory, it must be made clear whether we are talking of the theory in its simplified form as found in elementary textbooks or an adjusted long-term theory. It is plausible that the last model is most in harmony with actual pricing, but it cannot be readily used as a descriptive theory, because it is vague and imprecise. Furthermore, how can outsiders know whether firms are following a short-term or long-term policy? Hence, it is only fruitful to discuss whether the simplified form of the marginal theory is adequate.

It can often be observed that attempts to maximize profit are focused on the short term. The energy is concentrated on solving the acute problems here and now – whereas a solution to the long-term problems have to be found later. In my opinion, an assumption of short-term profit maximization will often be fairly realistic. Of course, this observation alone is far from sufficient evidence of the adequacy of the theory. Evidence has to be found as to whether pricing in practice agrees with the theory.

For example: if there is a change in price elasticity, will price be adjusted correspondingly?

If turnover changes, while price elasticity is unaltered, will price be kept constant?

If marginal cost is changed, will price also be changed?

If there is a change in fixed costs alone, will current price be maintained?

If the price elasticity is lower for A than for B, will the contribution margin for A be higher than for B?

In chapter 2 we briefly discussed how the theory should be understood. The theory requires determining the optimum price. This is not so in practice. Managers are satisfied if they can find a fair approximation or rather are able to determine the range of prices that will be acceptable.

In an actual situation, it might be difficult to determine whether a price is in harmony with the theory.

Let us illustrate the problem by an example of a chocolate manufacturer. He sells chocolate bars at a retail price of 1.25 dollars.

I asked him, "What would be the likely effect of a price increase to 1.35 dollars?".

He answered, "It would hardly affect sales!"

I then asked, "What about a price of 1.15 dollars?"

He replied that he would probably sell the same.

My next question was naturally, "Why don't you increase the price to 1.35 dollars?".

He was not able to give a distinct reply to this. He had on various occasions raised his prices successfully and sales were hardly affected. Thus, we have a manufacturer who believes that demand is inelastic, and all of his former experiences confirm this point of view. Still he does not increase his price! He would not accept the explanation that this was due to long-term considerations. The major reason was uncertainty. Until now he had been successful each time he raised his prices. But would it also work the next time? Another reason could be found in ethical considerations. Ethics play a great role to business executives; they are inclined to believe that it is unethical to increase a price unless "necessary".

This leads us to discover the paradox that the smaller are the chances for perfect correspondence between theory and practice, the higher the profit of the firm. When overall profit is unsatisfactory, the acceptable optimum area is narrow. The firm is forced to squeeze as much profit as possible out of each situation. The chocolate manufacturer could find himself in a situation in which he felt that he had to run the risk of increasing the price to 1.35 dollars. If the profit level is satisfactory, why run the risk of a price increase with a degree of uncertainty? He can afford the luxury of paying attention to other factors instead of only finding solutions to the most pressing problems.

It is obvious that the central question of whether real prices correspond to the theoretical prices is extremely difficult if not impossible to answer. You could imagine a research program in which you constructed demand and cost curves in a number of cases and thus determined the theoretical optimum price, which you then compared with the actual one. But this method is excluded. The problem is not only to determine the relevant curves empirically, but the curves are different under different assumptions. There will not be one but several optimum prices. You might find cases in which it is obvious that the price under no condition can be optimum. But a determination of the theoretical short-term optimum price will only be possible under special circumstances. Thus, it might be possible in case of monopoly. The analysis of the roller coaster price presents a unique example of the determination of the optimum price.

It is impossible to analyze systematically whether actual prices are equivalent to the theoretical optima, and if not, whether they are higher or lower. It is impossible to arrive at a conclusion that can be proved. But through your observations, you can form an opinion that might be more or less probable. I underline that the following conclusions are based on my own impressions and cannot be proved. But they can be supported by a number of strong arguments.

My first conclusion is that, if you compare actual prices with the short-term optimum prices of the elementary models, *there is a systematic tendency for actual prices to be lower than the theoretical optimum prices.* Several of our previous examples are in agreement with this. Thus, for the chocolate manufacturer it is probable that he was selling below the optimum price. As to the roller coaster price, it was almost certain that it was below the optimum level. The deterrent case is a more dubious example. You may take the point of view that the introductory price was much lower than the theoretical short-term optimum price, but the last one was purely theoretical and could never have been realized.

A number of considerations support this view. The marginal theory is immoral.

It determines the price that maximizes profit, irrespective of whether it is fair and just. But sometimes the optimum price implies an exploitation of a situation of scarcity, and many forms of price discrimination are a challenge to any feeling of fairness. But few firms want to be called exploiters and accused of immoral pricing methods. The concept of a fair price plays a role but will often not be in harmony with the optimum price. This point of view may play a greater role for big than for small firms. In 1991 the British medical company GLAXO introduced the product Immigran as an effective new medicine against migraine. The product was introduced at the same price in all countries – but the price was so exorbitant that it created a sensation the world over. Reactions were violent and the company heavily criticized. In Greece the product was simply not permitted. Of course I cannot prove it, but obtainable information seems to indicate that the price may very well be close to the optimum, as there is no doubt that demand is inelastic. Thus, it creates an uproar when a company tries to actually set the optimum price. This is an extreme case, but it may be an indication that firms usually do not dare to squeeze the highest profit out of their market.

A fact that supports this view is that there is a systematic tendency to underestimate the requirement of price elasticity for a price cut to be remunerative. As demonstrated in chapter 2, if a retailer operates with a mark-up of 20%, a 10% reduction in price requires a 60% increase in the number of units sold in order to be remunerative. Even though this is simple arithmetic, this condition is often overlooked. In practically all cases in which it has been possible to estimate price elasticity, the optimum condition is not fulfilled. According to the price elasticity, the optimum price is higher than the price set. You can even find cases in which the result of the analysis is a price elasticity below 1, which indicates that the price can be increased without delay. This is in harmony with the observation that, when you ask managers about their idea of the demand curve, they will nearly always indicate a price elasticity, which would make it rational to increase the price.

Simple observations indicate that, in certain situations, the price must be below the optimum. When there is a waiting line of customers trying to obtain a specific product, this must imply that a higher price could be obtained. For popular hotels it is sometimes impossible to obtain a reservation in the top season six months ahead.

The observation that there is a tendency for prices to be below the optimum has a number of consequences. If costs increase it is clear, in theory, that if it is an increase in fixed costs, it should have no influence on price. And if it is an increase in variable costs, the consequences for price depend on the demand curve. Normally, the price should increase by less than the cost increase. But you can observe that actual business behavior is not in accordance with the theory. Thus, prices often increase by the same amount as an increase in variable costs. The theorist will label such behavior as irrational. But if the current price is below the optimum, you can safely increase the price. And in the same way it may make sense to use an increase in fixed cost as a motivation for higher prices.

When economic theory is to evaluate the price effect of a certain change, it is usually done under the assumption that the relevant firm finds itself at the optimum in the opening position. But as this assumption may be unrealistic, the conclusions and predictions of the theory will also become unrealistic. Examples of this will be given in section 3 below.

An analysis of the relationship between actual prices and long-term optimum prices is more difficult, because the long-term optimum price is not a clear concept. Let us first consider a firm in a monopolistic situation.

Some of the arguments for the hypothesis that prices are below the optimum in the short term also hold for the long term. This applies for the inclination to underestimate the requirements to elasticity for a price cut to be remunerative. And the wish not to exploit any situation may also be relevant for long-term considerations. Thus, for the hotels, it would not have harmful effects in the long term to charge higher prices in the high season. And in the roller coaster example, it seems likely that higher prices would be profitable – also in the long term.

But the conclusion is not as clear as for the short term. It might be that the current price is below the theoretical short-term optimum, but that for various long-term considerations, it would be wise to keep the price.

It might be that the concept of a long-term optimum price is diffuse in the monopoly case, but it is far more difficult in a competitive situation. What the optimum price is depends on the reactions of actual as well as potential competitors, and there will normally be uncertainty as to their expected behavior.

Of course, the possibility of potential competition may be almost impossible to evaluate.

3.2 Explanation of relative prices

The subject in section 1 has been whether the absolute prices can be explained by the marginal theory. Another problem is whether it is able to explain the relative prices. Why is the price for product A higher than for product B? According to the theory, differences in price elasticities are reflected in corresponding differences in price. And if a mark-up system is used, the highest percentage mark-up should be applied to the products with the lowest price elasticity.

Numerous examples of this can be found in practice:

- In flower shops, mark-ups are higher for roses than for tulips.

- Automobile spare parts have a higher mark-up than the automobile itself. Also mark-ups are higher on the repair parts normally paid by insurance companies than on parts paid by the customer.

- The prices offered in the printing industry hardly include any profit, in the hope that the customer will ask for alterations and additions. These extras are priced so that they contribute to the profit.

- Mark-ups are lower on products for which the customer pays than on products paid for by somebody else, such as the government or a company. This principle is clearly illustrated in airline price structures.

Thus, many observations are covered by the marginal theory.

The point of view that no firm wants to be accused of exploitation influences the relative prices. Thus, different forms of price discrimination are often open to criticism. This plays a greater role for big than small firms. Especially the well-known firms often have to defend their price policy and explain to the public that their prices are not excessive. Thus, it plays a role in itself that a price can be defended. Whether the explanation is correct or not is of minor importance.

But this has the consequence that prices may be closer to their theoretical optimum than you would conclude from the explanations given by the firms. A few examples:

- A timber merchant charges higher prices to do-it-yourself enthusiasts than to professional carpenters. This discrimination is in agreement with theory, as the private customers lack the knowledge of prices that the carpenters have. Asked by a newspaper to explain this difference in prices, the timber merchant answered that servicing the private customers was more time-consuming, as they often need advice. The explanation did not reveal the real reason for the price difference, but it sounded convincing.

- A leading newspaper advocated stabilization of the wage and price level while, in the same period, it increased its subscription prices by 16%. The real explanation was that prices were clearly below optimum. But the explanation it gave was that it had suffered a decline in advertising revenue and had to compensate for this loss of income by higher subscription prices.

The concept of equilibrium is of general interest in economic theory. A system of price relations is in equilibrium if the condition that marginal cost equals marginal revenue is fulfilled for all products. If this is the case there is correspondence between theory and practice, as all price relationships are determined by marginal cost and price elasticities. If the condition is not fulfilled, can we assume that there are forces that will move the entire system towards equilibrium? If that is the case, the theory will have a certain predictive value. In many cases such a tendency can be found. Let us use a few illustrative examples:

Newspaper advertising

We have already mentioned a special case of newspaper advertising. Let us now take a more general view. Until a generation ago the pricing system was simply a certain price for each column-centimeter. In an economic sense this system was not in equilibrium, because no regard was paid to the fact that there were differences in price elasticity. The pricing procedure slowly moved towards a system that was more in accordance with theory. Now the price structure is highly differentiated. Thus, the price for advertising jobs offered is about twice that of the price for jobs wanted, because it is obvious that there is a difference in price elasticity. The least price sensitive is official announcements, which now carry the highest price of all. Today the price system is more in harmony with theory. However, ethical points of view play a role. Thus, the rate for death announcements is low, because it is considered indecent to charge a high price.

Coffee retailing

The development of the retail price for coffee in Denmark over the last hundred years offers an illustrative example of the working of market forces. Until the First World War, the retail price of coffee was remarkably constant, although there were violent fluctuations in the wholesale price. In some years retailers had profit margins of 300-400%. According to marginal theory, you would expect competition to have forced the profit margin down. It is astonishing that this did not happen, but the explanation must be that competition was not effective, due to tradition and the absence of brand names, among other reasons. It is more difficult to explain why the tradition continued between the two world wars and even in the time immediately after the Second World War. Coffee was definitely the most profitable item for the retailer, and the situation was so stable that the high earnings permitted a number of specialist coffee shops to exist. But this price system was not in accordance with the theory.

For many years it was certain that it would pay to compete on the price of coffee. Coffee is now sold under brand names, customers are mobile and supermarkets have expanded. A drastic price reduction had to come. And it did. Within a few years the entire system broke down. Gross margins rock-bottomed, and special coffee shops were no more economically viable. Thus, coffee retailing is an example of a tendency towards equilibrium, even though it took time.

Discount stores

Different forms of discounting can be observed in most countries, and discount stores have become commonplace since the Second World War. The predictive value of marginalism as a descriptive theory is recognized in the fact that the emergence of discount stores was predicted before the first store was opened. Prices were not at their theoretical equilibrium. Some products were more remunerative than others.

No single store had an advantage as long as they all carried a wide range of products with a range of contributions. This made it tempting to open a store with the remunerative products only – and omit the rest. By concentrating on the most profitable products, the discounters have forced the prices to be more in harmony with theory. It is probable that, if existing stores had theoretically correct prices, discount stores would never have appeared.

The theory also emphasizes that due regard must be paid to demand relations between various products. In principle, this has always been accepted by retailers, but only the most obvious relations have had consequences for price. It is not until recently that this principle has been carried through to its logical extent. Progressive retailers can be observed selling selected products below their purchase price. Not as a temporary remedy, but as a permanent part of their pricing policy.

These are not unique examples. It can often be observed that equilibrating forces are so strong that there will be a tendency for a system to move towards the theoretical equilibrium. In such cases the theory has a predictive value.

But is this equilibrating force so strong that it is possible to conclude that there will be a general tendency for all relative prices to be in harmony with the theory? Unfortunately, it is not. It is often observed that relative prices are determined by a rule of thumb. These rules give a more or less standardized formula for determining the relative prices, and there is a priori no guarantee that its application will result in prices that are in agreement with the theory.

3.3 Reaction to changes

If the marginal theory is to be acceptable as a descriptive theory, it has to be able to explain the consequences of changes in the basic factors.

The first eventuality is a change in the competitive situation. This possibility is so important that it deserves a full chapter (see chapter 6).

Another possibility is that a firm experiences a change in demand. Let us, for example, imagine that a firm notices a decline in demand and observes that fewer units are sold at the current price. If we assume that marginal costs are constant the theory states that this change should result in another price if the demand change involves an alteration of price elasticity, but not if it is volume alone that is affected.

If the reason for the change is a general decline in the number of customers, it might be that price elasticity is unchanged, and there is no motivation for a price change. But if the reason is that marginal customers have given up the product, leaving only loyal and faithful customers, price elasticity is likely to be lower and a price increase motivated. And finally, if the change is due to intensified competition, price elasticity may become higher and the optimum price lower than before.

Many reactions in practice are not in harmony with this theory. The theory assumes that the manager is aware of the causes for a change in demand. Sometimes they are so obvious that the manager is in no doubt as to what is the correct decision. At other times a manager only has a vague idea of the reason for the change and then there is no real motivation for altering the price. But in practice it can often be observed that the firms take action on price. A decline in demand is noticed as a decline in sales. This fact alone may induce management to act: "Something has to be done". "The decline must be stopped". "And quickly". And the quickest remedy is a price cut. In many cases this is not consistent with marginal theory.

In the opposite situation, when a firm experiences an increase in sales, it will normally keep prices constant, even though a price increase may be rational – at least in the short term. But the theoretical possibility exists that long-term considerations would dictate a lower price, for example, for deterrent reasons.

A third possibility is that a change in the cost structure occurs. According to the theory, it is decisive whether the change refers to fixed or variable costs.

Whether a change in fixed costs will influence price belongs to the next chapter on full cost pricing.

Here we shall treat the effect of a change in variable costs. As illustrative examples, we select a situation in which either a unit tax is imposed or a subsidy granted.

3.4 Effects of taxes and subsidies

The effect of a tax levied on a particular commodity has always been of interest to economic theory. The basic theory is illustrated in Fig. 3.1, which can be found in many elementary textbooks.

DD is the demand curve. With marginal cost constant, the optimum price is p_1. If a tax of t per unit is levied, the new optimum price is p_2. As the figure is constructed, the price will increase by one half of t. In general, if a unit tax is imposed, prices will increase by less than the tax, and if a tax is removed, prices will fall by less than the tax.

When a unit tax actually is imposed and the authorities or newspapers predict the effect on prices, they apply a reasoning that hardly can be called a theory. Government forecasts of the effect of a change in

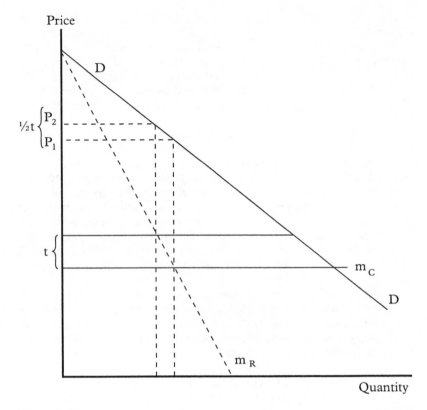

Figure 3.1

tax are normally that prices will change by the same amount as the tax. Who is right? The theory or the government? In most cases the government comes nearer to the truth than the theory, which implies that the theory is not useful as a descriptive theory.

It seems difficult to construct a descriptive theory, as there are great differences in empirical observations. A systematic collection of empirical examples would be a thesis in itself. Let us instead limit ourselves to a comparison of a few examples from Denmark in which direct taxes have been reduced.

On July 1, 1991, a special tax on perfume and cosmetics was abolished. Prices would have to be reduced by 34% to maintain the same profit margin. For the cheap products, prices were reduced by 34% or more. But for the more expensive imported products, prices were only reduced by 25%. The likely explanation for this phenomenon is that, because of the high direct Danish taxes, the import prices were kept relatively low, as otherwise selling prices would have been too high. But the tax reduction gave the chance for an upward adjustment of these prices.

This observation is in harmony with the marginal theory but not "the government theory".

Another example is the tax reduction in 1989 on radios, television sets, refrigerators, videocassette recorders, dryers and other electrical articles. In the majority of the cases, the prices were reduced by more than the tax reduction. In less than 5% of the retail outlets, prices were not reduced at least as much as the tax reduction. It was also observed that prices were reduced proportionally more on the most expensive items.

And again in 1990, taxes on videocassette recorders and color television sets were reduced by DKK 610. The average reductions in consumer prices were DKK 1123 for videocassette recorders and DKK 1050 for color television sets.

It is impossible to bring these examples in harmony with the marginal theory. There may be various reasons for this discrepancy. One interesting explanation is that the theory has been based on assumptions that are not sufficiently realistic. Thus, we have assumed that the existing price is the optimum one. But, as previously mentioned, this assumption is highly doubtful; chances are that it is below that level, and then there is no risk in increasing the price by the full amount of the tax. Furthermore, our reasoning has been based on the assumption of a linear demand curve. But demand curves in real life are never linear. In all probability, an assumption of a constant price elasticity is more realistic. On the condition that the existing price is the optimum one, the price change depends on the price elasticity:

Elasticity	Price change
−1.5	3 times
−2.0	2 times
−3.0	1.5 times
−4.0	1.33 times
−5.0	1.25 times

Thus, no matter what the elasticity is, the price should increase by more than the tax and by more with a lower price elasticity. Correspondingly, a tax reduction should cause prices to drop more than the amount of the tax. Some of the observations may be in harmony with the theory – but not all. If a general theory should be selected, it can only be that prices simply are increased by the amount of the tax.

Another example is the price effect of a value-added tax (VAT), which is a form of taxation found in many countries. The theoretical effect of a VAT is more complicated than a unit tax, because the value added depends on the relationship between price and marginal cost. If the demand curve is linear, marginal cost constant and equal to the average variable cost, the value added in percent will be lower for a greater production volume. Thus, a VAT could influence the optimum price in theory but never in practice; the price is always automatically increased by the amount of the VAT.

A subsidy can be regarded as a negative tax. The motives for granting subsidies are more varied than the motives for levying taxes. Direct government subsidies may be applied to a product or group of products in order to benefit the consumers by lowering prices or to help the producers by stimulating demand and thereby production, or they may be used as a general anti-inflationary measure to keep prices down. It is interesting to notice that, whatever the motive, the authorities almost always expect that particular motive to be fulfilled.

General subsidies, as an anti-inflationary policy, have been tried twice in Denmark; it is of international interest to learn about the Danish experience.

In 1974 and again in 1976, the Danish parliament passed a law granting subsidies to all firms. The subsidy consisted of a specific amount per worker. The system was not combined with direct price control, but the government stated that the objective was to directly impact prices. In the debate, the government declared that it expected price reductions to be comparable to the subsidy.

According to the marginal theory, the subsidy would have some effect, because it could be regarded as a reduction in variable costs, as it was applied to wage costs, which are generally considered to be variable costs. And this would motivate a reduction in price.

But practically no effect on prices could be demonstrated. The main reason for this is that the firms did not consider the subsidy as a reduction in variable costs. It was paid as a lump sum with no guarantee that the policy would be repeated in the following year. Therefore, if a firm utilized the subsidy to decrease prices (or to postpone a price increase) this year, it would be difficult to implement the necessary price increase the next year if the subsidies were not continued. The subsidy did not provide sufficient motivation for the firms to adjust their prices.[18]

These two examples form thought-provoking illustrations of how catastrophic it might be when predictions of business reactions are entirely wrong.

The introduction of general subsidies is rare. A more normal motive is to stimulate demand. Let us use an example as illustration.

In the 1980s, the Danish Government wanted to encourage the use of alternative forms of energy, such as windmills, solar cells, etc. A system was introduced in which the government refunded consumers

[18] Although there were exceptions, most firms simply accepted the subsidy as a windfall income. One large company simply returned the check to the state with the remark that it did not need government subsidies. In another firm, the entire subsidy was used for a great – and highly successful – party for all employees.

30% of the purchase price of these products. A total of DKK 90 million was allocated for the first year of the project.

This policy was an instant success as the demand for alternative forms of energy, especially windmills, increased. In fact, the refunding policy was so successful that all the money budgeted for the project was spent within just three months. As everyone expected the subsidy to be repeated next year, the windmill producers received practically no orders for the next nine months. The net stimulus for demand was therefore doubtful.

But the interesting aspect of the program is its effect on the costs of windmill production. The manufacturers worked overtime for three months and remained almost idle for the rest of the year. An analysis was made to compare the actual costs of production with the same production evenly distributed over the entire year. The result showed that the cost per mill was higher under the subsidy program.

The medicine field offers a good example of the motive being to keep down the prices consumers have to pay.

In Denmark, the government policy of medicine subsidies has not been consistent. Sometimes a subsidy is paid on a specific product and at other times it is removed again. There have also been numerous changes in the size of the subsidy.

During a period in which some types of medicine are subsidized and others are not, prices should – according to the theory – increase most for those having obtained the highest subsidy. A detailed analysis shows that this is the tendency, but that the differences are smaller than they should be in order to be in accordance with the theory.

An example: on July 1, 1975, a number of products lost their subsidy or had it reduced. If the price index of January 1, 1975 equals 100, the price index for October 1977 was as follows:

	Price index
a. Products that lost a 75% subsidy	108
b. Products that lost a 50% subsidy	114
c. Products whose subsidy was reduced from 75% to 50%	112
d. Products without changes in subsidy	119

According to the theory, price increases should be lower the more the subsidy has been reduced. This was also the tendency.

We shall use another specific case as illustration. In chapter 6 we shall use the market for iron preparations as an example of oligopoly, as there are three producers. In 1973 a subsidy of 50% was granted to iron preparations. According to theory, the very existence of the subsidy should motivate a price increase from the three producers. But two of them did not react at all, whereas number three made a limited increase.[19]

As only number three is in accordance with economic theory, it is of interest to observe how the increase in price affected its sales.[20]

Year	Sales in millions of tablets
1972	3.9
1973	3.4
1974	3.5
1975	3.8
1976	2.9

There was no decline in sales in 1974 and 1975 in spite of the isolated price increase. Hence, price elasticity appears to be low, which makes the decision to undertake the price increase a rational one. It is likely that the price increase could have been even higher. But the higher the price increase, the greater the risk of some form of government intervention.

3.5 Conclusion

The conclusion is that the marginal theory *cannot* be accepted as a *general* descriptive theory. The marginal reasoning is based on the existence of marginal functions. But in a number of pricing situation such functions are irrelevant:

• When a firm submits a tender there are no cost and demand curves. Either they get the contract or not.

• Within certain industries it is possible to produce according to individual orders, for instance, in the automobile industry. This is made possible by the introduction of highly flexible computerized production systems. As each product is individualized, it is meaningful to talk about the marginal cost of each product, but not of a marginal cost curve.

• The elementary marginal theory is based on an assumption of a continuous production of identical products. But in our times other factors may be more relevant. Thus, we have mentioned that total costs

---

[19] It is interesting that, at the time, there was an economist in the management of the last firm but only pharmacists in the two others.

[20] Caution must be exercised when interpreting these figures because other factors have supervened. The explanation of the drop sales in 1976 was a lack of serious sales efforts during that year.

may depend more on the number of production runs than on the volume of production.

In its pure form, the marginal theory is based on the assumption of profit maximization. This assumption disregards business ethics. But a realization of the optimum price often implies exploitation of the consumers – which in itself is undesirable. This especially applies to the short-term optimum price. There is therefore often no correspondence between theory and practice.

It is perfectly possible to enlarge the simple theory by making more sophisticated assumptions. You can construct a marginal theory based on other assumptions than profit maximization. And first of all, you can replace the short-term theory with a long-term theory. But the very concept of the long-term optimum price is vague, and thus its explanatory value low.

The marginal theory gives a better explanation of the relative than the absolute prices.

The marginal theory has a certain value as a descriptive theory. It is able to explain many phenomena. Thus, if it is obvious that price relations deviate from the theoretical optimum, it will predict that equilibrating forces are likely to come into effect.

Thus, the theory can explain certain phenomena, but there are too many results that contradict the theory for it to be accepted as a general descriptive theory.

Let us see whether a full cost theory can do it better.

4. Full Cost as a Descriptive Theory

4.1 Definition of full cost

In chapter 1 we mentioned that, roughly speaking, all cases of pricing could be separated into three broad categories. One category consists of cases in which price is determined by demand alone. Another in which demand and cost factors play an equal role. And finally a category in which price is solely determined by cost factors, thus neglecting demand. This last category can be divided into a number of sub-categories.

The most important one is what we term *full cost* or *average-cost pricing*. There is no clear and comprehensive presentation that can be called the full cost theory.[21] It is just a name for a number of pricing procedures in which, in principle, all costs are allocated to individual products and thus are decisive for the final prices.

As the concept is very vague, a number of distinctions are relevant.

As to the formal procedure, two main principles exist. In the first variant, which is termed *mark-up pricing*, the calculation of price is based on average variable cost. The price is set according to the formula:

$$P = AVC + GPM$$

where
AVC = average variable cost and
GPM = gross profit margin.

The GPM consists of two parts:
AFC = average fixed costs and
NPM = net profit margin.

In the second variant, prices are based on average total cost. Normally this method is simply called full cost. According to this principle, the pricing formula is:

$$P = ATC + NPM$$

where ATC = average total cost.

$$ATC = AVC + AFC.$$

[21] Through time a number of authors have presented full cost points of view. For example: P.W.S. Andrews: *Manufacturing business*, London 1949; W.J. Eiteman: *Price determination. Business practice versus economic theory.* Ann Arbor, MI, 1949; and R. Barback: *The pricing of manufactures*, 1964.

It is difficult to give a precise definition of NPM. For example, it may be defined as the profit margin that yields a "fair" return on invested capital and covers all risks.

AFC is determined by dividing total fixed costs (TFC) by the level of output. There is considerable uncertainty as to what this output is; for example it may be "normal" or "budgeted" or "maximum" output. There is one basic difficulty connected with this concept. If it is a multi-product enterprise, fixed costs are likely to be indirect costs, which implies that the fixed (indirect) costs have to be assigned to each individual product after a process of allocation.

Another distinction is between rigid and flexible full cost.

Rigid full cost is the designation for a system in which all costs are calculated into the cost of each product according to a pre-determined process of allocation. The price is found by adding a predetermined percentage or absolute, net profit margin to the calculated ATC.

All other systems are termed *flexible full cost*. This flexibility may manifest itself in a number of ways.

One method is to add different net margins for different products. The margin may even be negative, so that the price is below calculated full cost (= ATC).

Another possibility is flexibility built into the calculation methods.[22] Different criteria can be used for different products. Thus, for product A overhead is added as 20% of labor costs, whereas it is added as 40% for B. A totally different system may be used for C, such as costs being determined as machine hour rates.

Furthermore, we must distinguish between *total* and *partial* allocation. In the first case, all types of overhead are allocated to the different products. In the latter case some but not all types of overhead are allocated. For example, production costs will be allocated, whereas general sales and administrative costs may not be.

4.2. The content of full cost

We shall first focus on the second variant, in which average total cost forms the basis for pricing, and clarify the idea of full cost and how it works.

If we accept the assumption, which is often made for industrial enterprises, that the short-term average variable cost has a flat stretch, we can

---

[22] In order to avoid misunderstandings I shall distinguish between two different categories of cost. The first is between variable and fixed costs, where the criterion is whether cost varies with production. The other is between direct and indirect costs; the latter are often termed overhead or general costs. Fixed costs may be direct: for example, the cost of a machine used to manufacture one product only. Fixed costs will more often be indirect. For example, when different products are manufactured on the same machine. Variable costs are often direct, such as when labor hours can be stated specifically for each product, but may be indirect if this cannot be done.

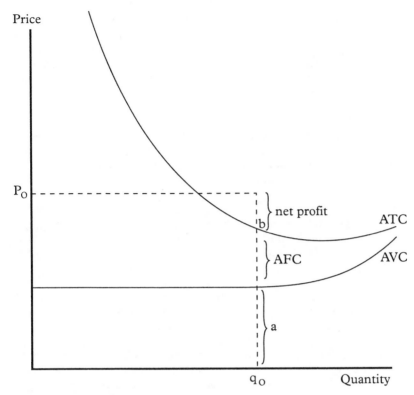

Figure 4.1

use Figure 4.1 as an illustration. The assumption is that not until full capacity is approached will the ATC begin to increase.

The budgeted or normal output is assumed to be q_O. AVC is a. To this is added AFC, which determines ATC at the point b. When the normal net profit is added to this, we arrive at the price p_O, which is called the full cost price.

For many business executives this price will be regarded as the "right" price, the "correct" price or the price they ought to charge.

Whether they actually can obtain that price depends on a number of conditions:

- It depends on competition. In case of monopoly there is, in principle, no hindrance for charging p_O. If there is actual competition it is decisive which form this competition takes. The situation may be that the business executive will sell nothing if he sets the price at p_O. But the existence of competition does not necessarily exclude full cost. Thus, in case of price leadership it is perfectly possible that the price leader bases its prices on full cost, whereas the followers are merely price takers. On an oligopolistic, heterogeneous market it is conceivable that pricing is dominated by full cost thinking. And on a market with many sellers, each seller may base his or her pricing on rules of thumb in which cost is the decisive factor. Or it may be that a trade association tries to enforce uniform prices, based on the full costing principle.

- It also depends on potential competition. If there are barriers to entry, it might be tempting to charge a price higher than p_O. Otherwise if the threat of potential entry is strong, the quoted price may be lower, for example, only covering ATC.

- It depends on the eventuality of government interference. If this is a realistic possibility it may involve a risk to charge prices above p_O. But it should always be possible to obtain this price, because the firm at any time will be able to "prove" that it is only getting a normal or "fair" price.

- It may depend on general economic conditions. In periods of depression, chances are that the price will go below the normal level. And the opposite when business is booming.

The motives for full cost. Full cost can be regarded as an attempt to determine prices by cost only and to discard demand considerations. The obvious reason is that the demand curve is conceived as too vague and elusive to form the basis for price determination. But that is not the only reason:

- Ethical points of view may play a role, perhaps only as modifications in an otherwise profit-oriented system. But few managers like to be regarded as exploiters. The good old concept from the medieval church of *justum pretium*, the right price, still plays a role. The right price is one that covers all costs and provides a fair profit.

- Especially big firms are often in a situation in which they have to explain and motivate their prices – and especially their price changes. If a manager increases a price by 10% and a journalist asks why, the manager cannot answer that he realized that the price elasticity is lower than previously thought or that demand has increased. An acceptable answer is that raw materials have increased in price or that the workforce has received higher wages. Whether the explanation is correct is not decisive as long as it sounds convincing. Therefore, if the real motive is on the demand side, you have to wait until you can find a suitable excuse on the cost side.

A motive of special interest is that, although you consider the marginal way of thinking as well suited if the goal is short-term profit maximization, full cost is appropriate for maximization in the long term. So if you want to carry out a long-term policy, you should choose full cost.

The problem is whether the cost functions in full cost calculations should be interpreted as short-term or long-term functions. This point is treated (among others) by A. Koutsoyiannis[23]:

> "The firm looks at its long-run position and aims at the long-run profit maximization. However, given the uncertainty in the environment, the firm bases its price on the short-run AVC; the firm believes that its costs will not increase if it expands its scale (in the long run) and probably they will be lower than in the short run. Thus, the short-run AC is sought by business men to be a good approximation to the long-run average cost."

My own impressions do not substantiate this point of view. In the cases of full cost with which I am familiar, it was evident that calculations were based on short-term costs and with practically no considerations as to what costs would be in the long term.

But the very fact that also fixed costs are included in the price calculations may prevent a firm from trying to exploit short-term opportunities. Thus, compare two trades. In the first one, all are familiar with economic theory and apply marginal reasoning in a short-term sense. In the other trade all members are totally ignorant; they base their prices on full cost and are so ignorant that they will refuse an offer a little below calculated cost with the motivation that they do not want to sell at a loss. But the paradox is that the second trade will earn more than the first one!

How will full cost pricing be affected by changes in cost or demand?

A change in variable costs should manifest itself into a corresponding change in price. In principle, higher fixed costs should also cause prices to rise. A decrease in calculated AFC due to better utilization of existing capacity should leave prices unaffected if calculations are based on normal cost but motivate a price reduction if they are based on actual utilization.

A change in price elasticity should not influence prices. But it may be accompanied by a variation in demand volume. Increased demand will lead to a better utilization of existing capacity and should, as just mentioned, permit a reduction in price. This is not normal practice, however. Firms usually leave prices unaffected and eventually adopt a queuing policy – at least temporarily. Correspondingly, a decline in demand should lead to a price increase according to a consistent full cost reasoning.

---

[23] Citation from A. Koutsoyiannis: *Modern microeconomics*, MacMillan, London, 1975, p. 273.

4.3. The existence of full cost

The basic questions are how widespread full cost thinking is in practice, which forms it may take and how consistent systems of full costing are. But there is an additional question. It might be that fixed costs have an influence even in cases that cannot be characterized as consequent full cost. It may be only on special occasions, only for one category of fixed costs, or only for some prices and not others. Thus, it is of interest to obtain an impression of the role fixed costs play in practice.

Rigid full cost may be an exception – but it does exist. Thus, examples can be found on markets with strict government regulation, due to the absence of competitive forces, for example, monopoly or collusion.

It is an interesting observation that big multinational corporations sometimes have made serious attempts to enforce rigid full cost on a world-wide basis. There are various motives for this. One is that such companies are almost constantly in the limelight. They have to defend their prices not only to the public but also to government investigative committees. And in any country it is a strong argument that prices are calculated in exactly the same way as in all other countries. Another motive is that the central control with the many subsidiaries is facilitated if the same strict system of cost calculation and price setting is used everywhere. However, more and more modifications have been made to this rigid policy for the simple reason that competition has become stronger on some markets than on others.

Rigid full cost is an exception, but even on competitive markets you may find examples. But only temporarily, because a firm stubbornly using full cost is apt to die, sooner or later. As just mentioned, you will run into the vicious circle of full cost: sales decline. The allocated cost to each unit is consequently increased. This gives as a result higher prices, which cause a new decline in sales, and so on.

Examples: a hotel had its annual rent increased. The proprietor reacted by increasing his room prices. The result was a decrease in the number of guests so that the final result was a drastic decrease in annual income.

A retailer lost sales because of competition from a discount store and reacted by increasing prices – with a serious decline in sales as result.

But you cannot automatically conclude that the circle is "vicious". In the hotel example, the reaction of the hotel proprietor was irrational. But if his prices had been below the theoretical optimum, he would have gained by the price increase. This possibility can be illustrated by an example: the total circulation of a ladies' weekly had declined. Based on a full cost line of reasoning, the price was increased. The result was that the weekly circulation dropped from 120,000 copies to 80,000, but the profit increased!

When full cost is used, it normally is applied with some degree of flexibility. Full cost can be observed in a great number of variations, and it is impossible to present all existing forms. In the following we shall limit ourselves to present some typical examples.

But before doing that, we shall make the general remark that fixed costs often influence on business executives' way of thinking. According to the marginal theory, fixed costs should not influence price, but in practice they do. The examples are so numerous that you just cannot discard them as exceptions. A few typical examples:

- In 1990 in Madrid, Spain, there was a recession in the building industry and it was difficult to obtain remunerative prices. However, one of the biggest construction companies was able to give a relatively cheap offer because it was in the fortunate situation that it owned a building lot that had been bought and paid for several years ago.[24]

- In Copenhagen the normal rate for local telephone calls is DKK 0.375 per minute, but in a hotel it can cost up to DKK 0.74 for a local call. The normal rate for a long-distance call within Denmark is DKK 0.70 per minute, but in a hotel the charge may be as high as DKK 3.90 per minute. M. Beier, the president of the Danish Association of Hotels and Restaurants, justified the discrepancy on May 9, 1986 to *Politiken*, a leading Danish newspaper:

  "The high prices can be explained by differences in the hotels' expenditure on telephone installations. Different rates between hotels are explained by how recently the hotel installed its system. It may be a modern and expensive system or an old installation. The alternative to high rates for using the telephone would be for the cost of the telephones to be spread among all the guests in the form of higher room rates."

- The rooms in a hotel in a Danish provincial town have a small refrigerator. If guests take a beer from the refrigerator the hotel charges them DKK 22. In the bar they can obtain the same beer for DKK 15. The difference was explained as the costs of the refrigerator that had to be covered, and as few guests actually bought beer from the refrigerator, the price naturally has to be high.[25]

- A company used the circumstance that a machine was fully depreciated to give an especially low offer in a competitive situation.

[24] Author's personal visit to the company, 1990.
[25] Personal information from Bent Friborg Henningsen.

4.4 Illustrative examples

Example 1. Publishing houses

An example of an industry dominated by full cost thinking is the book-publishing houses.

Traditionally this industry has been influenced by non-economic points of view. For the publisher, social, cultural and idealistic considerations play an important role. Throughout time, the publisher has been forced to adopt economic points of view in order to survive. It is an oversimplification to suggest that the goal is profit maximization. Publishers are aware of their cultural responsibility and may choose to publish a book that they know will cause a loss. They feel an obligation to publish it and hope that they will reap sufficient profit on other books. But the forces of competition compel the publishers to take account of economic considerations. Otherwise they are competed out of the market.

Pricing has always remained a mystery to the publisher. Some publishers have experimented with different pricing procedures and have normally suffered disappointment, as they often gave unacceptable results. There is not one method of pricing that is adhered to by all publishing houses, but there is a system in common use, and many publishers follow this at least as the main rule.

This system is summarized as follows.[26]

Costs are separated into 4 categories:

1) Costs that vary with the size of the print run, such as paper, printing and binding. These costs can be regarded as proportional to the number of copies printed.
2) Direct fixed costs, which are related to a specific book but are independent of the number of copies, such as typesetting, copyediting and proofreading.
3) Indirect fixed costs, such as rent, heating, salaries, sales and advertising expenditures.
4) Costs that depend on price and number of copies sold. These have two components: authors typically receive royalties of 15% of the price, and bookstores traditionally have gross margins of 35%.

VAT is added to these four categories of cost.

The starting-point for this price procedure is to ask the sales department how many copies of a particular book it expects to be able to sell. Let us assume that the answer is 2,000.

---

[26] The publishing house sets not only the price the bookstore has to pay but also the final selling price to the consumer, thereby determining the bookstore's profit margin.

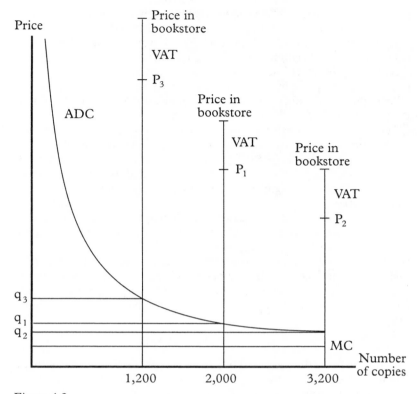

Figure 4.2

The next step is to calculate the proportional costs per copy; this can be done fairly accurately. This is represented by the line MC in Fig. 4.2.

Then the total direct fixed costs are found. When this amount is divided by the number of copies you have the direct fixed cost per copy. This added to MC gives the curve ADC (= average direct cost) in Fig. 4.2. With an estimated sale and printing of 2,000, this gives the point q_1. Thus, q_1 is an expression for the direct cost of printing the book. This figure is then multiplied by 5.

Why 5? Because it is common experience, substantiated by statistical analysis, that the selling price in the bookstores, minus VAT, consists of the following elements:

Technical cost (= ADC)	20%
Royalties to author	15%
Advertising	5%
Indirect fixed costs	15%
Profit and risk margin	10%
Bookstores' gross margin	35%
Price (excluding VAT)	**100%**

AS ADC constitutes 20% of the selling price, you can simply determine the price by multiplying ADC by 5 and then add VAT.

If the price, as a result of this calculation, were always adhered to it would be a case of rigid full cost. But that is not what normally happens. Based on the information of a sale of 2,000 copies, the calculated selling price is p_1. This price may be chosen, but what often happens is that the sales department informs you that it can sell 2,000 copies. But not at the price p_1.

What will the publisher do then? There is no definitive answer, as it varies from publisher to publisher and even from book to book.

A typical reaction is that the publisher decides to print a higher volume, for example 3,200. ADC is reduced to q_2, and now comes the crucial point: When this figure is multiplied by 5, the much lower price of p_2 is achieved.

It may end up that the price p_2 was a good approximation to the theoretical optimum price, and the sales estimate was correct, as 2,000 copies are sold – but 3,200 copies are printed.

I have observed a few cases in which the publisher is smarter than that, basing the calculation on a volume of 3,200, thus arriving at the price p_2. But the publisher then "cheats" and manufactures only 2,000 copies. The actual price, p_2, may be an approximation to the optimum price.

Is it likely that it will be?

The formal procedure is based on cost. Demand factors are not entirely absent. In a situation in which it is obvious that a calculated price deviates from the optimum price, the selling price may be regulated upwards or downwards.

Furthermore, a distinction is made between different categories of books. It is a common experience that price elasticity is high for children's books. Thus, normally the mark-up for this type of books is relatively low, even though a formal full cost procedure is applied. But the principle is not consistently carried through. Thus, the price elasticity of university textbooks is generally low. But publishers choose to apply a "normal" mark-up on these books. This attitude may not only be due to ethical reasons but also to avoid criticism from students.

There is one more peculiar reason why demand and cost factors may be intertwined. When the consumers know that the volume of a particular book is low, they expect the price to be high – and are willing to pay it. Otherwise they will expect high volume to be connected with low price – and consequently their price elasticity will be higher!

Thus, we can observe the influence from demand factors, but not in a consistent and systematic way. They are only minor modifications in a system of pricing based on cost. Thus, we are presented with a variant of the full cost method that gives results that are different from what a strict application of incremental reasoning would give. No interpretation of the facts can give harmony between full costing and marginal reasoning!

Example 2. The paint and dyestuff industry

Price calculations have traditionally created problems in this industry. The major reason is that the production process is often complicated and it is difficult to allocate costs to separate products in a logical way. Even labor costs are often treated as indirect costs, as the same worker may simultaneously take part in more than one production process. On the other hand, it is obvious that some products contribute more to costs than others.

The fact that the industry has traditionally been dominated by technicians also plays a role. Technicians are inclined to adopt a full cost point of view: "The problem is to calculate as correctly as possible the true cost of each product." It is no wonder that the industry is highly influenced by a full cost way of thinking.

The dominant method is to apply a system of "equivalents". There are variations from firm to firm, but the central idea is the same.[27] In principle, an equivalent is an estimate of how difficult a particular product is to produce. Oil ground paint is often chosen as a unit with the equivalent figure of 1, as it has a fairly simple process of manufacturing.

Putty involves the lowest cost and has the equivalent of one half. The factor for synthetic enamel varies from 4 to 6 as result of a more complex production process. Even more complicated products such as inks, offset printing inks and colored newspaper printing inks may have factors ranging from 9 to 12. The value of each equivalent is found by dividing total indirect costs by the aggregated number of equivalent units. When the unit equivalent is known, the cost of each product can be calculated.[28] When the same percentage is added for net profit, it appears to be a system of rigid full cost.

But this impression is misleading. What may happen can best be illustrated by a hypothetical example. Imagine that green synthetic enamel is estimated to have an equivalent of 6 units. As the value of the unit is known, the cost price can be calculated and, with an addition of 10% for net profit, the calculated sales price is determined. It becomes apparent that the product will not sell at that price or at any price that covers calculated production cost.

What can you do? You could drop the product. As a result, the total number of production units is reduced. Then the value of the unit equivalent becomes higher and thus the costs of all other products are increased. Furthermore, if you want to maintain a full range of products, you cannot drop a product as important as green enamel.

You could choose a selling price lower than calculated cost, which implies that you add a negative net profit. Managers do not like to operate with negative figures and especially not for the item labelled profit.

---

[27] The presentation here is based on B. Fog, *Industrial pricing policies*, 1960.
[28] The system is more complicated than this, but the description is sufficient to understand the system.

The solution is obvious and tempting. You simply reduce the equivalent from 6 to 5, and if that is not enough reduce it further to 4. Thus, the calculated cost of green enamel is reduced, the product shows a profit on the balance sheet and everyone is kept happy.

In principle the equivalents are technically determined. But they are influenced by demand factors to a certain degree.

4.5. Rules of thumb

We have previously mentioned that the use of rules of thumb is widespread.[29] It is impossible to give any statistical figures on what percentage of all prices are determined in that way. But they play a sufficiently great role to motivate special treatment.

A rule of thumb may have its basis in demand: for example, when a firm's entire price policy consists of the rule: leading brand minus 10%.

But the great majority are determined from cost. Full cost may be regarded as a form of rule of thumb. Thus, also for such rules, a distinction can be made between rigid and flexible systems. If the system is flexible you do not necessarily accept the result indicated by the rule, but you may have various motives for adjusting it.

The reasons for the use of rules of thumb are obvious:

- To business executives, the process of pricing is often considered as a sort of mystery. They are really in doubt. Doubt as to how to treat different costs, doubt as to whether the consumers will accept their prices, doubt as to competitor reactions and doubt as how to make differences between products. They need a firm position – and find it in a rule of thumb.

- With a great number of products, you simply have to apply a more or less mechanical formula to determine prices.

- The practical setting of prices may be delegated to subordinates. They need firm guidelines on how to determine prices.

Let us start with a description of some typical rules of thumb.

The first example is the setting of prices on hotel rooms. The use of mechanical formulas is widespread. Thus, in the United States hotel industry, the most common approach is the Hubbart formula. This formula can be regarded as a prototype of rules of thumb, because its goal is to find a room rate that will cover all costs, including that of providing a reasonable return on the company's invested capital. That really is

---

[29] See, for example, W.J. Baumol and R.E. Quandt, "Rules of thumb and optimally imperfect decisions", *American Economic Review*, 1964.

what all managers are dreaming of. The formula involves the following eight steps.[30]

1. Calculate the desired profit by multiplying the desired rate of return by the owner's investment.

2. Calculate the pre-tax profits by dividing desired profits by the hotel's tax rate.

3. Calculate all fixed charges and management fees.

4. Determine all operating expenses.

5. Credit the income from sources other than rooms.

6. Calculate the rooms-division income required to cover all costs and to provide a reasonable return on capital.

7. Determine (a) the number of room nights available to be sold and the (b) estimated occupancy rate, and then calculate the number of rooms you expect to sell by multiplying (a) times (b).

8. Determine the appropriate room rate by dividing the revenue required to cover all costs by the number of rooms expected to be sold.

It would be wonderful for any hotel manager if this formula really worked! But built into the system are all the traditional drawbacks of any full cost system. Thus, it will lead to price increases in times of depression. Room rates in the 1970s and 1980s increased more than the Consumer Price Index. Many American hotel managers have tried to use the system, but the experiences are so bad that it has obtained the nickname "Hubbart the horrible".[31]

The need for workable guidelines must be great, since similar methods are in use in other countries. None of them are fully satisfactory, which is not surprising, as no regard is paid to consumer attitudes and competition. An important point is that the prices thus calculated are the official prices. But most customers pay a lower price. It is not unusual that 90% of the customers obtain a discount. And there are such considerable differences in these discounts that you may maintain that prices are determined through a process of bargaining. Customers making a reservation in due time may get a discount, but it also happens that individual customers comes in from the street and obtain a reduction – if there is idle capacity. Many big hotels have a sales office in the

---

[30] For a more detailed presentation of the Hubbart formula, see Michael M. Coltman, *Hospitality management accounting*, New York, 1987.

[31] An alternative approach based on traditional theory is presented in Elmer Roth: "How to increase room revenue", *Hotel Management*, 1955.

airport. Every day a list is sent to this sales office with especially attractive offers and lower prices if more capacity is available.

Still, rules of thumb play a role in the hotel industry, even though the system is perforated by a number of other considerations. The crucial problem is whether these adjustments go so far that a rule of thumb is modified to such an extent that the prices may be in harmony with the marginal principles. This is not likely to be the case. The modifications are seldom made according to a consistent plan, but are made in order to avoid the most glaring drawbacks of a rigid system.

An example of special interest for the theory is the pricing of wine in Danish restaurants.

Restaurateurs have a selection of high-quality wines and a choice of cheap wines. They have perfect knowledge of the marginal cost of each bottle as it simply is the purchase price. But they need a system that can guide them to the selling price. Two systems are commonly used. According to the first method, the selling price is found by multiplying the buying price by a factor between 3 and 5. The most exclusive restaurants will choose the factor 5 and maintain that this is due to full cost considerations, as higher operating expenses (rent, light and service) are incurred and necessitate higher mark-ups. And they will believe it themselves. But an alternative explanation is that the customers of the exclusive restaurants are less price-conscious than the clientele in the more modest restaurants.

The other method consists of adding a fixed amount irrespective of purchase price and quality. This implies that the price differences between various qualities are much lower than indicated by the first system. Until a few years ago the adding method was hardly used, but it is being used more and more, and it is estimated that, by 1990, 35% of all restaurateurs adopted this procedure. When restaurateurs are asked why they have converted to the adding system, they will answer that it is because it gives better results. This is so because they can observe that, in recent years, the customers have become more price-sensitive. An application of the multiplying method will give as a result that the high-quality wines are too difficult to sell. Thus, demand considerations adjust the method of pricing in the peculiar way that the price-setter selects another rule of thumb! But if interviewed, the restaurateurs will maintain that their prices are not influenced by demand. In all probability, none of the systems will lead to optimum price relations. It might be that quality wines will be priced too high by the multiplying method but too low by the rival system. The problem for the restaurateur is to find the rule of thumb that gives the best results, in other words, that come closest to the theoretical optimum.

The pricing methods of Danish goldsmiths constitute an example of price determination hardly affected by demand considerations. The goldsmiths have a calculation list. It is separated into three different categories of goods. When they know the purchase price, they can find the selling price in the list. The list is so detailed that it contains several hundred price intervals for each category, the mark-up being different for each price range. Almost all goldsmiths use the same calculation list, and they rarely do not charge the indicated price.

The result is that there is no price competition between goldsmiths in Denmark.[32] A modification has to be made. In recent years a few goldsmiths have started more keen competition, especially on price. The other goldsmiths have felt some effect, but not to the extent that they have given up their traditional way of price determination.

4.6. The controversy between marginalism and full cost

The marginal principle is formulated as a clear and consistent theory, but the same cannot be said about full cost.

We have mentioned in section 1 that, through time, a number of authors have presented different forms of full cost theory. But full cost has mainly been brought forward as a protest against the marginal doctrine, postulating that the marginal theory was purely academic and with little connection to the real world. The controversy was especially heated in the first decades after the Second World War. "The fight was spirited, even fierce. Thousands of students of economics, voluntary or involuntary readers have been either shocked or entertained by the violence of some of the blows exchanged."[33] Although the conflicting views are not as sharply formulated today, the conflict has never died out.[34] Nowadays a number of economists do not regard the controversy as a serious one, because they believe that it is possible to conciliate the two conflicting theories.

Thus, Machlup already arrived at the conclusion that the full cost and marginal theories may be completely compatible. They present different methods for determining the price, but with proper interpretation it might very well be that they only present different ways of arriving at the same end result.

We shall now try to give an answer to the crucial question: is there a relevant difference between full cost pricing and the marginal theory? Is it possible to interpret and modify the two theories in such a way that harmony can be obtained?

[32] This is in contrast to some other countries. Thus, in England there really is competition, also on price.

[33] F. Machlup, "Theories of the firm: marginalist, behavioral, managerial", *American Economic Review*, March 1957.

[34] It will carry us too far to present the historical development and to quote even the most prominent of the economists who have taken part in the debate. For a fairly detailed presentation of the development of the marginalist versus full cost controversy, see Frederic S. Lee: "The marginalist controversy and the demise of full cost pricing", *Journal of Economic Issues*, 1984, p. 1107. Machlup, "Theories of the firm: marginalist, behavioral, managerial", *American Economic Review*, March 1957.

Let us treat the two variants of full cost separately and begin with the first variant, in which a gross profit margin is added to AVC, in other words, mark-up pricing. As a good representative for the point of view that harmony is obtainable we can choose A. Koutsoyiannis[35]:

> "Even if one accepted that long-run profit maximization is the single goal of the firm, average-cost pricing would not be a new theory of the firm, since it can be proved that the same long-run equilibrium would be reached if one applied marginal analysis in the long-run. We will prove that setting the price on the basis of the average-cost principle involves implicitly the (subjective) estimation of demand in the long-run equilibrium position."

The "proof" is that if a firm applies the mark-up rule

$$p = AVC + GPM$$

and we apply the condition for profit maximization that:

$$p = AVC \, (e/e - 1)$$

we can deduce that:

$$p = AVC \, (1 + k),$$

> where k is the gross profit margin.

For example, if the firm sets a profit margin of 20%, by solving the equation we can determine the price elasticity to be (minus) 6. "Thus setting a gross profit margin is tantamount of estimating the price elasticity of demand and then applying the marginal analysis."[36]

But this analysis cannot be accepted as a proof. It is an example of backward logic, in which you start by assuming what should be proved: that the firm has actually obtained the maximum long-term profit. The only thing she can conclude is that the possibility exists that k is influenced by the price elasticity. But that does not necessarily imply that this is also the case in the real world.

A real proof would require that it is possible to determine that the price elasticity in the above case is (minus) 6.

I will regard a statistical analysis as excluded. Only in exceptional cases will it be feasible simultaneous to determine profit margin and price elasticity.

---

[35] Citation from A. Koutsoyiannis, *Modern microeconomics*, MacMillan, London, 1975, p. 273.

[36] op. cit. p. 280.

Another method would be to ask the relevant questions by mailed questionnaires. But you cannot expect business executives to have a precise idea of such an elusive concept as price elasticity. It is even doubtful whether they can explain how demand considerations influence their price-setting.

Actually you can prove nothing. You have to limit yourself to vague conclusions based on observations and impressions. But even your own impressions will never be so precise that you dare to state that the price elasticity is (minus) 6. At the highest, you can have the feeling that price elasticity is higher for product A than for B. But you will hardly ever be able to express the differences in quantitative terms.

The only thing you can do is to relate your own impressions – knowing that others may have received other impressions. And you will hesitate to generalize, because you have a great number of examples that contradict each other. But there does not seem to be any other way.

Let me try to relate my impressions. As to the absolute prices, I can only repeat what was said in chapter 3, that if you compare gross profit margins with an estimated value for price elasticity, many prices are below the optimum. If you ask business executives for an estimate of price elasticity, they will invariably indicate a (numerical) value that is so low that the above equations do not square. But it is doubtful whether you really can make this conclusion, because price elasticity is such a vague concept.

As to the relative prices, we have also in chapter 3 given many examples of how relative prices are influenced by price elasticity. But it is just as easy to find examples in which they are not. My own impression is that, when the differences in price elasticity are pronounced, there will be a tendency for prices to be adjusted correspondingly. At least in the long term.

My personal conclusion is that there is a strong tendency for gross profit margins to be influenced by price elasticity. But the tendency is imperfect. And first of all, you have absolutely no guarantee that not only the qualitative but also the quantitative relationships are in agreement with the theory. In my opinion, it is not admissible to draw the general conclusion that there is compatibility between mark-up pricing and the marginal approach.

Let us continue with the second variant of full cost, in which a net profit margin is added to calculated ATC.

We have previously mentioned that, in principle, perfect harmony with the marginal principle can be obtained by a sufficiently flexible system of net margins. Theoretically, it will be possible to add exactly the margin that leads to the optimum price. But this would imply that, in many cases, the net margin would have to be negative – and there is a deep-rooted psychological resistance to calculate with negative margins. Differences in net margins may be observed, but normally with differences much smaller than they should be according to the theory. Thus, compatibility with the marginal theory is unlikely.

In our presentation of full cost, we have time after time mentioned that demand considerations may creep in – often indirectly. It is a tempting hypothesis that harmony may be obtained if the cost allocation in reality is determined by price elasticity. Let us imagine a system that appears as rigid full cost, because all types of overhead are allocated to each product, and the same profit margin, such as 10%, is added to total unit cost for each product. Product A can easily be sold at the calculated price but not B. It is then tempting to find another system of cost allocation according to which a greater part of the overhead is allocated to A than to B. The process of reallocation may go so far that overhead in reality is allocated according to "what each product can bear". What the business executives call what the market can bear is what economists call price elasticity. If overhead consequently is allocated according to price elasticity, so the lower the (numerical) elasticity the higher the allocation of cost, and a constant net profit margin is added, you will arrive at exactly the same prices as by the marginal method – and full harmony is obtained. But again: the possibility that full correspondence may be obtained does not prove that it is also so in the real world!

In the paint and dyestuff industry, we found an example of demand-influenced cost allocation. Theoretically, it is possible that the reallocation of overhead is carried out so consistently that the end result is that there is full harmony with the optimum prices. But is it probable that it will be so? Once again you cannot prove anything, because you have not sufficient knowledge about price elasticity. But the fact that the procedure is not a consistent system, but a hodgepodge of different criteria make it unlikely that the theoretically optimum prices are realized. What is obtained are modifications in an otherwise cost-determined system.

Demand factors may be smuggled into an otherwise cost-determined system in many different ways. Sometimes demand and cost considerations may be so intertwined that it is difficult to get a true impression of the role each of them play. This mixing of demand and cost factors finds peculiar expressions. I have selected some examples:

- In a textile plant the profit margins are fixed, so that an adjustment to a changing market situation has to be done otherwise. It may, for example become apparent that a certain group of products are too costly. Production is rearranged so that these products are manufactured together with another group of goods that are less expensive to produce. This is not done to achieve cost savings, but rather to be able to calculate them together, thereby obtaining an average of cheap and costly products.

- In a radio and TV factory, for orders that are price-sensitive, the materials that have been bought at the cheapest price are used.

- To obtain a certain order, a paint factory estimated a batch on the basis of the hourly wages of apprentices, although most of the work had to be done by skilled and higher paid workers.

In the above cases, demand considerations can be said to be manipulated into the process of pricing. But even in cases in which no regard is paid to demand, prices may still be in harmony with marginal reasoning. Take the example of telephone charges in hotels. Telephone rates are higher than normal, especially in the more expensive hotels. But many of the guests are traveling executives who have their costs refunded and thus do not care about telephone rates. Their demand is inelastic. Thus, the rates may actually be in agreement with the marginal theory – even though the explanation is absurd from a theoretical point of view. But when interviewed, hotel managers will underline cost factors and not price elasticity – and they believe it themselves.

Hypothetically, rules of thumb may express years of experience and thus give an approximation to the right price. If the right price means the theoretical one, this is not the case. The typical rule of thumb expresses a sort of wishful thinking. It is an attempt to determine what the price ought to be in an ideal world. But as illustrated with the setting of hotel room rates, you charge other prices when it is not possible to obtain the "right" prices. Thus, we have to conclude that, in general, the rules themselves will not give prices that are in harmony with the marginal principle.

The picture is confused. We have demonstrated that the real content of a system may be different from how it looks on the surface. Thus, many cases of full cost may, by close analysis and proper interpretation, be brought in agreement with the marginal theory. Does this permit the conclusion that full cost and marginal theory may be completely compatible? Definitely not. There are too many cases of full cost in which demand considerations are either absent or only give such minor modifications that not even the most liberal interpretation can bring them in harmony with marginal reasoning. Thus, we have to conclude that full cost is a way of pricing that plays a role in itself and may be in contrast to the marginal theory.

4.7. A general descriptive theory?

Let us repeat that, in principle, we can construct three different descriptive theories:

- a theory that explains actual prices by demand factors alone

- a full cost theory

- a marginal theory.

The two main problems are:

- Can one type of theory be accepted as a general descriptive theory?

- Will it be possible to combine the theories or do they mutually exclude each other?

We can group all cases found in the real world along a horizontal line according to the role played by demand and cost factors:

Cost 100%				Demand 100%
Rigid full cost	Flexible full cost	Cost and demand of equal importance for price	Price determined with some relevance of cost	Price determined with no relevance of cost

You can imagine many different forms of price philosophy being placed in the middle group, but our exclusive interest is attached to only one: the marginal theory. As you can observe actual cases of pricing falling within each of the 5 groups, it is doubtful whether it is possible to construct one general descriptive theory. Either you can select one theory that can explain the majority of cases and regard all other examples as exceptions, or you have to work with more than one theory.

Full cost may be able to explain *absolute* prices better than short-term marginal theory. Incremental reasoning is better suited to explain *relative* prices. Full cost will never be able to explain why the contribution margin is higher on roses than on tulips. Only marginalism can give an explanation of price discrimination.

Full cost may be able to give an adequate description of the pricing of big *dominant* firms but rarely that of small firms. A firm with a minor market share has no use for a full cost calculation, because it knows that the market determines the price. Furthermore, the small firm will hardly ever have to explain its prices to public authorities or journalists, whereas big firms must prepare themselves for that eventuality.

Full cost may have a certain explanatory value within *industry*, but is of no relevance for *retailing*, not to mention *agriculture* and *fisheries*.

Marginal theory may be appropriate in relation to *short-term* pricing, but when *long-term* considerations dominate, a full cost explanation may be more appropriate.

It must be desirable for economic theory to be able to present one general theory. Is that possible? And if it is, which of the three alternative types is most appropriate? It is somewhat of a paradox that the debate has been marginalism versus full cost. It is likely that the theory that is able to explain most actual cases of pricing is the third alternative: the demand theory. This is in accordance with a long tradition. Already Aristotle explained that a thing could obtain a price because there was a need for it. It was its utility and not its cost that gave it a value.

Or to quote a representative from the school of Salamanca, Luis Saravia de la Calle (1544):

> "Those who measure the just price by the labor, costs and risk incurred by the person who deals in the merchandise or produces it, or by the cost of transport or the expense of traveling to and from the fair, or by what he has to pay the factors for the industry, risk and labor, are greatly in error, and still more so are those who allow a certain profit of a fifth or a tenth. For the just price arises from the abundance or scarcity of goods, merchants and money, as has been said, and not from costs, labor and risk. If we had to consider labor and risk in order to assess the just price, no merchant would ever suffer loss."

A great number of prices can be explained satisfactorily by demand factors alone. This is the case on highly competitive markets. But also the prices of followers in a situation of price leadership are set without any regard to cost.

In chapter 3 we concluded that the marginal theory is not well suited as a descriptive theory. A great number of observations are in agreement with the theory, but there are so many that are not that it is not permissible merely to treat them as exceptions. In addition, the marginal theory is vague and imprecise because marginal revenue as well as marginal cost may be interpreted in many different ways. In classroom examples, marginal cost and price elasticity are clear concepts. But not in the real world.

Can the full cost theory do better? In my opinion it is poorer! I do maintain my point of view that full cost considerations play their role. And some phenomena are best explained by way of full cost. But more observations can be accounted for by the marginal than by the full cost theory, for the simple reason that demand factors in most cases do play a role. Therefore it is natural to forward the argument that, if the marginal theory can explain more than the full cost theory, why not stick to the former theory?

This attitude is worth discussing. A good starting-point can be found in a quotation from A.G. Papandreou[37]:

> "I should be willing to give up my rational-action tool kit if the advocates of nonrational behavior models could either establish a high degree of invariance for the standards and rules of thumb they claim business firms employ, or offer a theory that accounts

---

[37] The quotation is from A.G. Papandreou's comments to Richard B. Heflebower's presentation of "Full costs, cost changes, and prices", in *Business concentration and price policy*, Princeton, 1955. National Bureau of Economic Research.

for changes in these standards and rules of thumb. Until they do either one of these things, the economic theorist may disregard their attack upon his methods of theory construction."

Thus, his point of view is that we have to stick to the marginal theory as long as a really convincing alternative theory has not been elaborated.

What is the aim of the theory according to Papandreou? Let us quote again[38]:

> "The task of the theorist, as I see it, is not to "explicate" reality; rather, it is to construct analytical models that permit him to predict reality. This implies the need for operational concepts and operationally meaningful propositions – propositions that is, which refer to empirical data. It is not sufficient for us to "account" for observed patterns of business behavior. We must be in a position to make a prediction about business behavior."

As chapter 1 demonstrates, my attitude is that the theory should be able to do both: to explicate and to predict. But I agree with Papandreou that the test for any descriptive theory may be its ability to predict.

It is an obvious objection to Papandreou's point of view that, if you choose the marginal theory as *the* descriptive theory, many of its predictions will be wrong.

Papandreou's entire argumentation is based on an illusion: the illusion that it is possible to establish *a general descriptive price theory*. When you have the entire range from 100% cost-determined to 100% demand-determined prices in the real world, it is impossible for one theory to cover everything. Some phenomena can be explained by one theory, but others have to be accounted for in other ways. Therefore, you cannot conciliate the full cost and the marginal theory. They are different. Under certain conditions one theory will give a reliable prediction; in other circumstances another will have to be used. But a general theory does not exist.

We have already mentioned some of the fundamental difficulties for any descriptive theory in chapter 3. It is a theory developed by outsiders, and how can they know whether short- or long-term considerations are relevant? And how can they know whether the goal is profit maximization or something else?

Thus, the present status for economic theory is that *it cannot present a general descriptive price theory*. This situation is highly critical. And it is not acceptable that the predictive value of the theory is as low as it is.

What shall we do? We have to admit that the pricing process takes so many different forms that no single theory can explain it all. Then we have to work with more than one theory. We have to establish a form of *typology*. It should be possible to work out a number of different price models and state under which conditions one or another type is relevant. The typology should result in a sort of catalogue describing different types of price behavior and stating under which conditions they are likely to be relevant. Thus, in the publishing industry, a price model that states that price depends on category of book (fiction, textbook, children's book and so forth), number of pages and number of copies printed will give a satisfactory explanation of actual pricing – and will even have a predictive value. The marginal theory may give a satisfactory prediction in certain situations; for example, the phenomena of discount stores was predicted before they started. But if you venture to predict the price effect of unit taxes, the marginal theory will mislead you.

4.8. Efficient prices

The fact that the traditional marginal theory is not acceptable as a general descriptive theory has a number of consequences.

It is not always made clear whether the marginal theory is used in a normative or descriptive sense. An important example is *welfare theory*. The central idea is the Pareto optimum, which can be considered a total social optimum. In a market with perfect competition, this optimum will be the result of the action of the "invisible hand". Prices that fulfill the Pareto optimum are normally called *efficient* (or fair) prices. If existing prices do not correspond to these efficient prices, it is a natural aim for government policy to try to influence and regulate prices so that an approximation to the ideal situation is achieved.

In a perfect market, the Pareto optimum is achieved if all prices are equal to marginal costs. *But the Pareto optimum is a theoretical abstraction of no value in the real world.* If all prices were equal to marginal costs, all firms would go broke, as their overheads are not covered. Furthermore, if some products are sold on a perfect market whereas others are sold under monopolistic or oligopolistic conditions, the Pareto optimum is not realized. In principle, it might be possible by some form of regulation to achieve this, in other words, find the prices that would exist if there had been perfect competition on all markets. If the market for product A is perfect, whereas there is a monopoly for B, resources should be transferred from A to B. The regulator could achieve this by granting subsidies to the consumers of B and instead put a tax on A. Some customers will be worse off and others better off, but until the Pareto optimum is realized it will be theoretically possible for the gainers to compensate the losers for their loss – and still be better off. This is highly theoretical because, in practice, it seems impossible to imagine that such a compensation scheme would ever work.

Naturally, welfare theory recognizes that many markets are imperfect. But practically all welfare theory is based on the assumption that, irrespective of market form, the behavior of the firms is in accordance with the marginal theory. But this assumption is not realistic! The theory is usually understood as a short-term theory. If we have markets, and marginal cost is interpreted as short term in one and as long term in the other, there can be no equilibrium in the Pareto sense. The same holds true on the demand side. The theory takes it for granted that there is *one* demand curve. But as previously underlined: for any product at a given time there are a number of demand curves, each defined under special conditions.

Even though the basic welfare theories are theoretical in the extreme, the very line of thought is of interest. And in order to make the theory more workable, the elementary theory has been expanded to cover more realistic assumptions. A number of economists have contributed to this development. A model that is relevant for us is the following. Let us assume that a firm manufacturing two services (= products) is working under the restriction that profit has to be zero. The best Pareto solution is that prices equal marginal costs, but this does not fulfill the constraint that profit equals zero, as overhead is not covered. But it can be demonstrated that the second-best Pareto solution that fulfills the conditions is obtained by the *Ramsey prices* (also called Baumol-Bradford-Ramsey pricing).

The basis for Ramsey pricing is that you make the assumption that the goal for all firms is zero profit, for example, that all costs have to be covered. If you replace marginal pricing by full cost, the idea in Ramsey pricing is that the maximum efficiency of pricing is realized when overhead (assumed to be equal to fixed costs) is allocated to each product in inverse relation to price elasticity. The lower the price elasticity of a particular product, the higher the percentage of overhead allocated to that product.

For any two services, we can imagine such an exploration for a "Pareto superior" price adjustment, given any initial set of prices that has the firm at zero profit and given that prices throughout the rest of the economy are maintained at marginal costs. The Ramsey prices are the zero-profit prices for which there is no Pareto superior adjustment. That is, at the Ramsey prices the firm satisfies its zero profit constraint and, further, any slight price adjustment that maintains it at zero profit will result in aggregate gains being exactly equal to aggregate losses. Ramsey prices are thus economically efficient in the sense that there is no way that they can be adjusted to benefit some without harming others.[39]

A diagrammatic construction may be helpful to understand the idea of Ramsey pricing.[40] Our firm working under the constraint of zero profit has two markets, Service 1 and Service 2. Assume that the demand curves for the two markets are the straight lines $D_1A_1D_2$ and $D_3A_2D_4$.

Ramsey prices are indicated by p_1 and p_2 respectively. For these prices the relation D_1A_1/A_1D_2 is equal to D_3A_2/A_2D_4. Furthermore, the sum of the overheads is equal to total overhead, so that the constraint of

---

[39] Quoted from Edward Zajac, *Fairness or efficiency*, Massachusetts, 1978.
[40] The diagram is reprinted from Zajac, op. cit, p. 28.

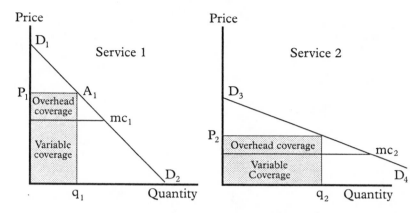

Figure 4.3

zero profit is fulfilled. But the criteria for allocating the overhead between the two services is price elasticity. The lower the price elasticity of a product, the higher the proportion of overhead allocated to it.

It is interesting to compare this theory with our observations on flexible full cost. We have found cases in which full cost is practiced so that the allocation of overhead is influenced by price elasticity. But that really is Ramsey pricing. In the majority of flexible full cost, overhead allocation may be independent of market conditions, but the profit margin may be determined by price elasticity: the lower the elasticity, the higher the profit margin. Also this situation is in harmony with the Ramsey principle. Instead of being regarded as the second-best optimum solution, this principle might be said to be the best, because it has the advantage that all costs are covered, in contrast to the true Pareto optimum.

Thus, we arrive at the interesting hypothesis that a *general use of full cost pricing is superior to marginal pricing because it has better chances of leading to efficient prices.* A general system of marginal pricing may lead to the short-term optimum. But for all practical purposes, it is more relevant to determine the prices that will be most efficient in the long term. And then it might very well be that a general system of flexible full cost is to be preferred. But it is obvious that, if full cost pricing is dominant in some markets and marginal pricing in others, there is no total equilibrium in the Pareto sense.

If welfare economics has to be taken seriously, it is about time that it be based on the actual behavior of business – and not on unrealistic theoretical assumptions.

5. Full Cost as a Normative Theory

5.1 *The merits of full cost*

A hypothetical explanation of why management often rejects a marginal approach and prefers a system of full costing might be that management is ignorant of the marginal theory. It is undeniable that this is often the case, but it is not a sufficient explanation, as you can find managers with an advanced degree in economics who consistently apply full cost methods. They simply regard the marginal approach as insufficient.

Imagine an industrial entrepreneur who introduces a new product. The price has to be set.

How much guidance will he find in the marginal theory?

This depends on the competitive situation. If the new product is a close substitute to existing products, he may choose to reason along marginal lines. He may simply decide that the product will be brought on the market if the obtainable price covers marginal costs. But if the product really is an innovation, the situation is different. The sellers do not know the demand curve. They might have a vague idea about (short-term) price elasticity but are fully aware that it may be different under different assumptions. They may have a fairly good idea of marginal costs, which they understand as short-term marginal costs. But they are fully aware that these constitute only a small fraction of the total cost. They simply feel that marginal reasoning is too imprecise to give sufficient guidance. They look for more substantial support. They may resort to a rule of thumb. Or they may try to seek guidance in a full cost approach.

Managers feel that they are on firmer ground if they can start by calculating the total average cost of the product, which is another expression for full cost – even though they may be aware of the arbitrariness of that concept. In order to calculate ATC they have to know the volume of production. Typically, they will do this by making an assumption of normal or average capacity utilization. Therefore, calculated full cost will depend on assumptions. Actually, full cost only represents a more or less arbitrary point on the ATC curve. However, the full cost is only the starting-point for their deliberations on price selection. The calculation will give them an idea of what price level to aim at. But this starting-point will be moderated by demand considerations, which are consistent with the marginal theory. Thus, full cost forms the backbone of the pricing procedure, whereas the marginal points of view come in as modifications. The net profit margin will be adjusted according to a feeling of what the market will bear. This margin could be negative if the manager realizes that the product will not sell at a price corresponding to full cost.

The marginal approach is invariably superior to full cost under the condition of perfect information. Without perfect information, there are a number of reasons why managers prefer a full cost to a marginal approach.

The first reason is practical in nature. We have previously mentioned that, in many firms, a large number of prices have to be set.

They need a routine for price setting. Below in section 2 we shall, as an illustration, mention the construction of a normative system for the printing industry.

The second reason is related to the organizational way prices are determined. In elementary textbooks, one person sets the price, and this person has a perfect knowledge of demand as well as cost. In a firm above a certain size, prices are typically determined through cooperation between different departments.

Market information is accumulated in the sales department and cost information in the accounting department. Frequently, the final decision on price is made in the marketing department based on a cost calculation from the accounting department. One possibility is that the cost calculation includes only direct and variable unit costs or even marginal costs. Experience shows that this usually results in a price lower than what a full cost procedure would lead to – and probably also lower than the theoretical optimum price.

The marketing department focuses on selling, and of course it is easier to sell when you can quote a low price. The other possibility is to present the marketing people with a full cost calculation. The marketing department will need strong arguments to propose a price below calculated full cost. But of course there is no guarantee that the final price will be anything close to the theoretical optimum.[41]

The third reason is more sophisticated. Management may want to base its decisions on long-term marginal costs, i.e., all the future increases in costs that may be caused by the introduction of the new product. As an estimate of these costs is considered difficult or even impossible, present full cost may be regarded as an acceptable approximation.

It will always be difficult to demonstrate a clear relationship between total future costs and the (present or future) volume of production of the new product. Nevertheless, there may be a relationship called *creeping indirect costs*. In a short-term marginal approach, these creeping indirect costs are simply ignored. In a long-term marginal analysis, management may try to carefully estimate all future consequences on the cost of the new product. But often management may find such an ap-

---

[41] The price will often have the character of a compromise. I have personally observed a case where the accounting department deliberately falsified its full cost calculations by adding an extra amount, because they knew that the selling department always wanted to reduce the calculated price. Hypothetically, the end result may be the optimum price – but it is not likely.

proach so uncertain or arbitrary that it is without value. It may therefore choose to regard present full cost as an approximation to future total costs.

A fourth reason is also of a theoretical nature: that full cost is regarded as an approximation to the value of the resources in their alternative best employment, in other words as *opportunity cost*. The approximation is based on the reasoning that, if product X cannot cover its share of total costs, it should not be introduced, because the profit obtained by adopting product Y would be sacrificed. However, this argument is not necessarily logical. If there is idle capacity, then adopting product X does not require any sacrifice. Also, if there is little spare capacity it might be a mistake to choose product X even if it is able to cover the overhead allocated to it because product Y might give greater returns.

The theoretically correct approach would be to reason by way of opportunity costs. Managers often find this procedure too complicated and difficult. Therefore, it is tempting to select a full cost method as a substitute or approximation to the theoretically correct method. But it must be underlined that it can never be more than an imperfect substitute.

A fifth reason is also illogical in principle: that full cost is a safeguard against being forced to lower your price. The price-setters are keenly interested in successful sales. If they received many comments from customers complaining about high prices, it would be difficult not to lower prices. In order to prevent a prohibitively low price, they need the moral support of the "price floor" that a full cost system gives them.

The sixth reason is also illogical in a way. We have previously mentioned that a crucial difference between theory and practice is *that the objective of theory is to determine an optimum price, whereas a primary objective of practice is to avoid making the worst mistakes*. Thus, management may very well realize that average-cost pricing does not necessarily result in the best possible price – but in a price that is acceptable.

5.2 Illustrative examples

Example 1: Publishing houses

In chapter 4 we used price-setting in the book-publishing industry as an example to illustrate full cost thinking. We shall now come back to the same industry, seen from a normative point of view. There may be different reasons for a full cost approach prevailing in the industry. A few decades ago, pricing within the industry was in chaos. Not only had the average publisher no knowledge of marginal theory, but he was not even able to make consistent full cost calculations. The pricing procedure was a game of guessing, with demand considerations as the main basis. But publishers systematically underestimated the requirements of price elasticity, so that many prices were too low. For many publishers prices could not cover all costs, and many of them went broke. In desperation, one publisher took the initiative to construct a system of calculation that was based on a full cost philosophy and could be regarded as a sophisticated rule of thumb. His system obtained wide acceptance and is still in use. However, some frustrated publishers have given up the method as unsatisfactory, obviously because it has the traditional defects of a full cost system, which does not take demand into due consideration.

But as stated in chapter 4, the pricing philosophy is still full cost, even though there now are a number of skilled economists in the industry: for example, the chairman of the trade has an advanced degree in economics.

What are the motives for a manager with perfect knowledge of the marginal theory deliberately to select a full cost approach? The publishers discard the marginal theory as insufficient. That is not tantamount to saying that they cannot see the fallacies of the full cost method, but it gives a more firm guidance than a purely marginal approach.

The distinction between direct and indirect costs is decisive. The arbitrariness of the calculation methods for indirect, fixed costs is acknowledged by the publishers.[42] But when it comes to direct, fixed costs such as typesetting and proofreading, there is a profound conflict between theory and practice.

Marginal theory is clear on this point: direct fixed costs influence whether a book should be published or not. However, if it is decided that the book should be published, these costs have no influence on price because they are independent of the number of copies printed.

No publisher accepts this line of argument. One thing that any publisher understands is that the larger the print run, the lower the unit cost per copy and the lower the final price can be. If you have two books with the same number of pages, the same costs of typesetting and no obvious difference in price elasticity, a consequence of the theory will be that they should be sold at the same price even though one of them is likely to sell 500 copies and the other 50,000. To the publisher, this seems absurd, as it appears obvious that the most popular of the two books can and should be sold at a lower price.

Publishers reject the theoretical approach as not sufficiently helpful. They know that marginal cost is only a small fraction of the total cost. They may consider paper as the only variable cost. But they reject right away the idea of setting the price based on paper costs alone. They may pay some regard to demand, but the notion of price elasticities for different types of books is too hazy to be helpful. They need a firm foundation for their price policy. They may find it in a full cost calculation, such

---

[42] The methods for calculating the costs determined by price, such as VAT, royalties to authors and bookstore margins, are not adequate. It is preferable to treat these costs as a reduction in the demand curve rather than as an addition to the cost curve.

as the one mentioned above. We have already said that a number of publishers have given up this system of calculation. Or it may be better to say that they have adjusted it.

Therefore publishers find that a price calculated on a full cost basis will be unrealistic, but at the same time they are reluctant to accept the consequences of a purely marginal policy of pricing.[43] From a normative point of view, it seems preferable to combine the conflicting systems. A full cost calculation may serve the purpose of giving an idea of the price level, thus forming a useful basis for setting the price. But it is evident that, in many cases, the full cost price has to be adjusted according to relevant demand factors.

Example 2: The printing industry

There are similarities as well as differences between this industry and the publishing houses. An important difference is that, within the printing industry, you have to work with two systems of prices. One possibility is that a given job is on firm order so that the customer afterwards is billed for the amount. This system is often based on many years of co-operation with the customer. Here marginal reasoning is not very helpful; you have to work with a fairly inflexible pricing method. The method does not necessarily have to be of a full cost character, but it must be consistent through time.

The other system is that the printer is asked to submit a tender for a specific job – often knowing that other printers also give their bids. Although many publishers are well acquainted with the economic theory, most printers are totally ignorant.[44]

The average printer feels a high degree of uncertainty in pricing. They need guidance – but cannot find it in marginal reasoning. Experience shows that even if they are tutored in the marginal theory, they are not able to apply it properly. It does not give meaning to talk about the price elasticity in each individual case. And if they try to apply the theory when submitting a tender, they are apt to use it incorrectly. They will understand the theory as saying that, if there is idle capacity, they are better off by obtaining the job at any price above marginal cost rather than miss the order. After some sad experiences they reject the marginal theory and takes refuge in a full cost calculation. And discover that they hardly ever obtain an order!

[43] One of the biggest publishers, after trying various methods of pricing without much success, got so frustrated that he adopted a rule of thumb. He simply weighed the books! He then had a scale: so much per kilogram for children's books, so much for textbooks, etc. He firmly maintained that this system gave results that were not inferior to more refined methods – and he saved all the calculation cost.

[44] This situation has changed somewhat in recent years, as the trade association has organized a number of courses to educate its members. It is of special interest that courses in price calculation are arranged.

And even in case of firm orders they run the risk that the customer once in a while takes an outside offer in order to control the prices.[45]

The trade needs guidance in its price policy. Economists within the trade have worked out a guide that seems to give a workable solution. What is important is that they have deliberately rejected the marginal principle as insufficient. In principle they have constructed their method as a full cost system. But the main idea is that it shall be possible to supplement it with a marginal approach. Thus, any calculation is a full cost calculation, but constructed so that you immediately can estimate marginal costs. The full cost calculation gives you information on the price you "ought" to take. The other of how low a price you can accept.

But the demand situation has to be taken into consideration. Even though each product is so unique that it has no meaning to talk about the demand curve in the traditional sense, it is well known that some customers are more price-sensitive than others.

To this naturally comes that due regard has to be taken to the competitive situation. In many cases the printer will have an idea of not only who else will submit a bid but also at what level the price offers will be. In spite of this, it is astonishing how great the variation can be among the bids for the same order. A difference of 100% between the lowest and highest bid is not uncommon.

5.3 Advantages and disadvantages of full cost pricing

If the requirement of a normative theory is that it should determine the "correct" price, neither marginal theory nor full cost can be accepted. It is characteristic for most pricing situations that the decision is influenced by a great number of factors. You cannot put all these factors into one simple formula. Normally the decision-makers are highly in doubt and need guidance in their deliberations. Therefore, instead of discussing which method determines the "best" price, it seems more fruitful to formulate the problem as: which approach gives decision-makers the best basis for their price deliberations? The marginal theory is constructed as a logical system. In practice, people can never refute the logic of the system, but they may find that it does not give them the guidance they want. And as previously mentioned, when substantial

---

[45] An illustrative example: a big printing firm (one of the few where the manager is well acquainted with economic theory) had satisfactory relations with their biggest customer for many years. This customer once asked for a bid from another printer and this offer was 23% lower. When confronted with this fact the first printer made the psychological error of replying that he would also be able to deliver at the lower price. The customer got angry, accused the printer of having cheated him over the years and broke all trade relations.

costs are not allocated among products there is a risk that it tempts management to set prices too low. According to McGuigan and Moyer[46]:

> "This can happen only if the firm lacks an effective control system in which one person continually monitors the overall contribution of a firm's complete product line. This person can then ensure that prices are set sufficiently high in relation to both the variable cost of each product and the total fixed cost of the firm. In addition, marginal pricing gives the firm far more flexibility in setting appropriate prices, evaluating offers to buy below this price, and comparing alternative uses for the firm's productive capacity. One may conclude that there is nothing full-cost pricing can do that marginal pricing, properly controlled, cannot also accomplish."

This statement is undeniably correct – if all business executives are fully informed and behave rationally. But the problem is that, in the real world, marginal pricing is rarely properly controlled. The person who is supposed to ensure that the overall contributions cover total costs is either lacking or not strong enough.

Therefore, the decision-makers may prefer to work with a system that is workable even though it is not 100% logical. In practice, methods can be found all the way from complicated and elaborate pricing models to homemade rules of thumb.

A special aspect of full cost is that its effect may be that of a price cartel. We can use the goldsmith trade as an example. As almost all goldsmiths use the same formula for price calculation, there is practically no competition on price. The members of the trade want to compete on quality, service and assortment, but not on price. If customers try to check that the price charged is fair, they will be reassured when they compare the prices offered in other stores.[47]

The entire process of pricing within the goldsmith trade is an inflexible system – and you can hardly find any traces of marginal reasoning. Would it be beneficial to the trade to scrap its old-fashioned methods

---

[46] Quoted from McGuigan and Moyer, *Managerial economics*, 5th edition, West Publishing Company, St. Paul, MN, 1989, p.551.

[47] That cooperation instead of competition is of great benefit to the trade is obvious, and sometimes finds peculiar expressions – which will surprise the theoretical economist. Thus, it happens that a customer offers a goldsmith some old silverware and asks for a price. The goldsmith offers a price, and often the customer replies that he or she will think it over. The goldsmith knows that the customer will proceed to the closest store and try to obtain a better offer. The first goldsmith telephones immediately to the closest colleagues and inform them of the price offer. When the customer actually visits the next goldsmith, he or she will receive exactly the same price offer – and will be convinced that it is futile to continue further research. This behavior has the character of a price agreement, but the goldsmiths within the same local region are convinced that, in the long term, all of them will benefit from this form of cooperation – instead of trying to overbid each other.

and introduce marginal reasoning? In my personal opinion: definitely not! The present system really functions as a price cartel, with all the advantages this gives to a trade.

Thus, under certain conditions full cost may be preferred to marginal reasoning. But even though full cost may have its value, it hardly ever is sufficient in itself. In most situations you cannot entirely neglect demand considerations but have to use full cost in a flexible way. Variants of full cost are sometimes marketed under brand names: for example, Scientific Pricing. Such a system may form the backbone of the pricing process and may give management a certain feeling of security. But this feeling may be an illusion.

As the full cost method is not logical, it is only natural that it can lead to wrong conclusions.

Examples have already been mentioned previously. One mistake is to refuse to accept a price below calculated cost for the reason that "I do not want to sell at a loss".

Another defect of a full cost system of allocation is that it may give management a distorted picture of the relative profitability of the different products. Product A may show a high percentage profit for the reason that its capacity is fully utilized, whereas product B figures with a loss because of low utilization of capacity. Based on this information, management may make serious efforts to promote the sales of A at the expense of product B, which is an irrational decision.

If full cost is to be of practical value, demand has to be taken into consideration, which implies that it has to be combined with marginal points of view. As mentioned for the printing industry, there are advantages in combining the two conflicting points of view. Basis is taken in a full cost calculation, which is then modified by demand considerations, partly to consumer behavior, partly to the likely reactions of competitors.

An example of an elaborate formula for pricing is that based on a target return on investment.[48] This principle is in reality a refined version of the simple full cost model by including an item for the acceptable rate of return on investment. This method has certain advantages for a firm in a strong market position, but has all the usual disadvantages connected with any type of full cost pricing.

---

[48] See A.D.H. Kaplan, J.B. Dirlam and R.F. Lanzilotti, *Pricing in big business*, Brookings Institute, Washington, DC, 1958.

6. Price Strategy in Competitive Environments

6.1 Different types of competition

In chapters 2-5 we have presented the full cost and marginal theories in a general way, without always specifying the competitive situation. But naturally the degree of competition has a decisive influence on the price policy of any company.

Traditional economic theory classifies competitive situations according to the number of competitors and whether the market is homogeneous or heterogeneous.

At one extreme you have *perfect competition*, in which each seller is confronted with a horizontal demand curve. On this market there is no doubt that the marginal theory is relevant, as each seller will maximize profit by producing as long as price covers marginal cost. The theory is relevant in a normative sense. But this does not necessarily imply that the behavior of firms always agrees with the theory. It can often be observed that firms produce beyond the equilibrium point.

At the other extreme you have *monopoly*. As a monopolist does not have to pay attention to competitors, there is no need for a modification of the discussion in the preceding chapters.

Hence only two market forms are relevant. One is *monopolistic competition* with many sellers on a heterogeneous market. The other is *oligopoly*. Of these, oligopoly is most interest in relation to price strategy. This will be understood as heterogeneous oligopoly, as there are almost always differences between the oligopolist's products.

The theory of oligopoly is usually presented in textbooks containing both descriptive and normative elements. Usually, a number of models are presented to show how the pricing process may unfold under various assumptions. As such, it is more a clarification of what might happen than a description of what actually does happen. It is descriptive in the sense that it states under which conditions a specific model is likely to be realistic. Normative aspects enter in the form of recommendations on what the rational behavior will be under specific conditions.

Typical distinctions are between:

1. *Homogeneous* and *heterogeneous* markets. Oligopoly in a homogeneous market is a theoretical abstraction of some academic interest;

2. The *number* of oligopolists – a special case is *duopoly* with two competitors;

3. The *degree* of substitution between the products of the oligopolists. A measure of this is the price cross-elasticities;

4. The *relative* strength of the oligopolists. A measure of this is their market share;

5. The *number* of products;

6. A *pure oligopoly* or a fringe of *small* competitors.

Further distinctions can be made according to the relationships between oligopolists. One extreme relationship is *collusion*. This might be a price cartel, a contingency cartel or some other form of agreement, and all of them may be open or secret.

In the case of no formal agreement, there is an important distinction between *autonomous* and *conjectural* behavior. In autonomous behavior, oligopolists do not consider the fact that their actions may influence the competitor's policy. If they do foresee it, they will act in a conjectural manner.

A special model is *price leadership*, which can take many forms. One form is when the followers set the same price as the leader. Another form occurs when the followers constantly undercut the leader.

A formal price agreement signed by the participants is a clear expression of collusion, but if they just meet and discuss business conditions they may influence each other without a formal agreement.

I am well acquainted with a number of oligopolies in Denmark. In all of these the members are in contact with each other. This might be at meetings of the trade organization but, more commonly, most contact is by telephone. However, this does not amount to making agreements, and it is possible to observe keen, even merciless competition although the members are in regular personal contact with each other.

We shall first consider the theory of oligopoly as a descriptive theory. We have previously stated two requirements of a descriptive theory: first that it be able to explain oligopoly pricing and that it have a certain predictive value. It must be stressed that it is not always possible to separate prices from other parameters of action. A change in price is thus often accompanied by a change in product quality or advertising.

The second question is the usefulness of the theory in a normative sense. How much guidance will an oligopolist who is going to set a price find in the theory?

In the economic literature, a great number of empirical examples can be found of oligopoly behavior. Thus, it is often possible in studies of special industries to find descriptions of oligopoly pricing. As a supplement to these I shall start by presenting illustrations from three different industries. In contrast to most other examples, these three cases are based on my own experiences and observations, which may not be representative but shows what might happen, which may give an opportunity to understand what has been going on. It is difficult to say whether my examples are typical, since we might well ask just what normal oligopoly behavior really is. One of the great difficulties of oligopoly theory is that you can find examples of almost everything. There are so many variations that it is extremely difficult to make a separation into different categories and seemingly impossible to formulate a general descriptive theory. But at least there is nothing extraordinary about the examples.

6.2 Illustrative cases

A case from the newspaper industry

In Copenhagen there are two large newspaper firms, Politiken (P) and Berlingske Tidende (B). The main products for both presses are a morning and a lunch paper. Over time there have been variations in the daily circulation, but they are always approximately equal. In some respects the competitive situation of Politiken and Berlingske Tidende is a duopoly, although far from a pure one.

The two firms have acquired an intimate knowledge of each other. Their behavior is a complicated mixture of keen competition and close cooperation. For example, they have mutual interests in relation to the public authorities and to other newspapers. The formation of a joint company for the distribution of the two newspapers is an expression of close cooperation. They have a gentleman's agreement that, in the case of a strike at one of the newspapers, the other will not expand its circulation. However, keen and even grotesque examples of competitive actions are easily found. Their behavior sometimes resembles athletes in a sporting match rather than managers in a rational business environment.

Our special interest is focused on the price competition between P and B. There are many different prices. One group is the advertising space prices. Another the price for buying a newspaper. We have to distinguish between the price for a single copy sold at a newsstand and the normal subscription rate. But subscriptions may have special prices, for example, special introductory discount prices.

The pricing process can be characterized as neutralized price competition. Both parties are keenly interested in increasing their daily circulation at the expense of the other but not with price as a parameter of action. There is no formal pricing agreement, but contact is always made before any price adjustment. Both parties realize that there is nothing to gain through an active pricing policy, as any competitive action will almost surely be neutralized by the other.

Once one of the newspapers was in a poor financial situation and management believed income had to be increased immediately. The easiest option was to increase the price. However, management hesitated to do this because it doubted whether the competitor would follow. Ultimately, the firm took the risk and initiated a price increase. The other newspaper did not follow and the result was such an alarming decrease in circulation that neither paper will take such a step again. A few years

later, the other newspaper was experiencing financial difficulties and
considered a price increase as a solution. This time management contacted the rival, but when it received the answer: "We do not need a
price increase at the moment", management felt that a price increase
was out of the question.

Two cases from the medical industry.

Each type of medicine can be considered to have a market of its own.
The number of suppliers for each category of medicine varies, but the
typical pattern is one of oligopoly with a few firms involved. For many
categories of medicine, the products from different firms are close substitutes, as their chemical content is approximately the same. In spite of
this, price cross-elasticities are often low, due to strong market positions
obtained through advertising, sales promotion and strong brand names.
We will now examine two cases of what happened when a new competitor tried to penetrate an oligopolistic market.

Case 1: chlorpromazine, a tranquilizer.

Fig. 6.1 shows the price of chlorpromazine in Denmark between 1961
and 1978. Up to 1972 there were only three products on the market, A,
C and D. The products could be regarded as close substitutes. There
was no formal price agreement, but typically the managers consulted
each other prior to the implementation of a price increase.

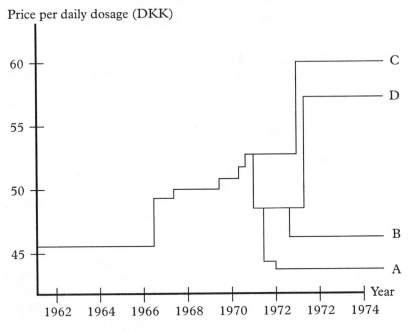

Figure 6.1

The interesting year is 1972, when peace was broken. A fourth product, B, was introduced on the market by a company that had decided to add this type of tranquilizer to its existing product line. It hoped to penetrate the market with a low price. As indicated in Fig. 6.1, the producers of A and D reacted immediately, reducing their prices to the level of B, whereas the producer of C ignored the challenge. Shortly thereafter producer A intensified competition by undercutting B. Two years later D changed its strategy with a dramatic price increase. This move created a market with two high-priced and two low-priced products.

The development of sales for the four products is as follows:

Annual sales (in thousands of daily doses)

	1970	1971	1972	1973	1974	1975	1976	1977	1978
A	190	160	92	30	42	31	16	0	0
B	0	0	149	217	255	315	322	322	328
C	347	274	192	204	153	139	118	112	108
D	925	835	875	835	800	830	750	760	795
Total	**1432**	**1269**	**1314**	**1286**	**1250**	**1315**	**1206**	**1194**	**1231**

It can be observed that:

• There has been no expansion in the total market. The four products are competing for a constant market.

• The strategy of B has been successful in the sense that it has secured a solid second position in the market.

• A is the loser, although it was A who met the challenge and intensified the competition on price. The explanation is that the profit margin was reduced to such a level that the product was no longer a priority for management. No sales efforts were made and, in 1976, the product was withdrawn from the market.

• As a consequence of its high pricing policy, C's market share declined in 1974 but not to an alarming extent.

• Throughout the entire period, D maintained its position as the leading supplier, although it suffered some loss of market share to B.

d. Case 2: iron preparations
The price trends from 1965 to 1976 are shown in the Fig. 6.2.

At the beginning of the period, only two products were in the market with the same price, N and Q. The first interesting year is 1965, when B (the same firm as in the first case above) entered the market with a low-priced product. N followed immediately, whereas Q decided on an en-

Price per day (DKK)

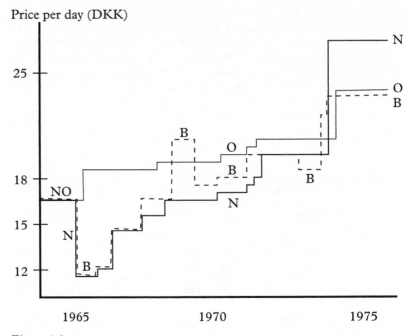

Figure 6.2

tirely different strategy and shortly afterwards increased the price. After 1965 the price trend went upwards, and in 1969 B was the most expensive product.

The second notable episode happened in 1973 when all three products received a government subsidy of 50%. The effect of this has been discussed in chapter 4.

e. A case from the detergent industry

The supply of detergents in Denmark is dominated by four companies, all of which are affiliated to multinational corporations. One of them, in the following named Blue, has as its main product a special type of detergent that holds a firm position on the market. The main interest focuses on the interplay between the remaining three, Red, Orange and Green, all of which have a full assortment of products. The products can roughly be divided into three segments – high, medium and low priced.

Within each group, the products from the different companies can be regarded as close substitutes. The grouping is not constant over time. A brand may move from the high price category into the medium group and vice versa. The same firm may have more than one brand within the same segment, for example, a special non-polluting product.

In addition to the Big Four, a number of smaller firms have sprung up selling in the low price segment only. Their brands are relatively un-

% Market share

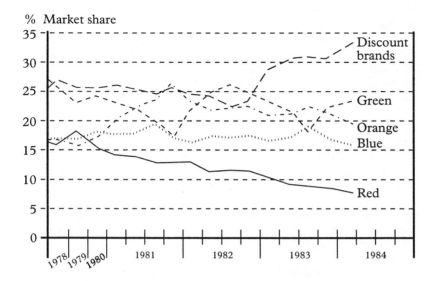

Figure 6.3

known, advertising is on a small scale, and their only effective parameter of action is price.

From a theoretical point of view, the main interest is the policy of the Big Four, who are approximately of the same strength and have a good knowledge of each other. The interplay between these four companies is made more complicated by the existence of the cheap brands.

A complete description of the development of prices would require an analysis of each specific product, which would take up an entire book. We have selected a specific period between 1982 and 1984 as being of particular interest. Fig. 6.3 shows the market share, for all types of detergents, of the Big Four and the smaller players.

During this period the small firms gained substantial ground, with a secure position of a combined 30% market share in 1984. Blue has a fairly stable market share due to the special character of its main product. Blue is therefore of limited interest in the following context.

The situation faced by the other three in the beginning of 1982 was not satisfactory. All of them had lost market share during 1981. A price war to drive the low-cost brands out of the market was not seriously considered by the leading companies, as such an action would be costly. Even if it were successful, the technical equipment and machinery would probably be sold for virtually nothing to somebody who would then begin to manufacture detergent.

Because of insufficient earnings, management was more inclined toward a price increase. No formal pricing agreement existed between the Big Four, but they kept regular contact, exchanged points of view and often, but not always, informed each other of their intentions along general lines – but never in detail. Therefore, around New Year 1982 they all expected a relatively small price increase. Such a step would have represented a typical example of coordinated action. But suddenly, and with only a few days notice, Green reduced prices dramatically. Technically this was done by moving a well known brand from the high price segment down to the middle group.

Green's annual report for 1981 was submitted to the parent company, showing a drastic decline in market share. Without further analysis, the parent company informed Green that this was unacceptable and that the market share of earlier years had to be regained in 1982. Green was convinced that the only way to obtain this goal was to drastically cut prices.

Green was successful in that the objective was reached. Green became the leading brand in 1982, but suffered the consequences of a transition from a small profit to a substantial deficit. If the goal was profit maximization, the policy was an absolute failure.

How did the others react? The low-cost brands did nothing. Their profit margin was already so low that it was hardly sensible to reduce prices further. They lost market share, but survived.

Red and Orange immediately dropped all plans for price increases, as they knew that they had to meet the competition on price. They could have achieved this in a number of ways. They chose to maintain their leading quality brands, introduce entirely new low-price products and to let medium-price products slide down into the cheap category. These steps turned out to be sufficient enough to prevent further reductions in market share.

The effects of these countermeasures on Green can be seen in Fig. 6.4.

The figure shows Green's total market share including the product reduced in price, brand A. Clearly it is product A alone that gained share, whereas the others lost market share. Fig. 6.4 also indicates that, toward the end of 1982, even A began to lose market share. This can be explained by the countermeasures taken by Red and Orange. By 1983, Green is back at the starting line. Green found a solution in the third quarter of 1983 by introducing a new high-quality product as a substitution for brand A, which was now placed in the medium segment. In the figure it is termed brand B. This step was decisive and the trend was reversed.

6.3 Oligopoly theory as a descriptive theory

Here I have related a few examples of price behavior in oligopoly. In addition to this, I have some knowledge of oligopolistic behavior in other industries, and the literature has many descriptions of oligopolistic behavior. The central question is whether all these different observations can be brought in harmony with the existing theory of oligopoly pricing.

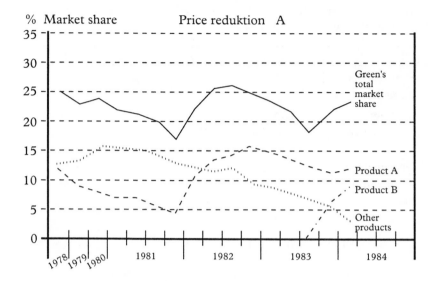

Figure 6.4

It is impossible to give a definite answer, as there is not one conclusive theory. Current oligopoly theory enumerates a number of different models and discusses under which specific circumstances each model may give a realistic description of the real world. There is an enormous literature on oligopoly, and new and valuable contributions appear in a steady stream.[49] Theory has always had a preference for the duopoly situation for the reason of simplicity. We shall follow that tradition and concentrate on duopoly theory.

We have to limit ourselves, as it is not possible to comment on all existing duopoly models. We shall start with what now may be termed the classical theories of duopoly, which are all characterized by being based on highly simplified assumptions.

The theory makes two distinctions: whether we have *homogeneous* or *heterogeneous* products; and whether *price* or *quantity* is the decisive variable. There is a tendency in the literature to begin with a homogeneous market and with quantity as the decisive variable. An illustrative model is presented by Hirshleifer.[50] Under the simplified assumption of an industry demand curve $P = 100 - (q_1 + q_2)$, where q_1 and q_2 are the quantities of the two duopolists, and zero costs, the different duopoly situ-

[49] A useful survey of the theory of oligopoly is given by P.A. Geroski, L. Phlips and A. Ulph, "Oligopoly, competition and welfare. Some recent developments", *Journal of Industrial Economics*, 1985. The following references to oligopoly theory are mainly taken from this.

[50] Here quoted from J. Hirshleifer, *Price theory and applications*, Prentice Hall, Englewood Cliffs, NJ, 1984, p. 297.

ations are shown in the following table. The profits of the two duopolists are indicated by Q_1 and Q_2 respectively.

	q_1	q_2	Q_1	Q_2
Symmetrical				
Collusive	25	25	1250	1250
Cournot	33.3	33.3	1111.1	1111.1
Competitive	50	50	0	0
Asymmetrical				
Pre-emptive	50	25	1250	625
Threat	50	0	2500	0

Collusion is the best option for the duopolists, as it maximizes total profit.

The second possibility is that the Nash-Cournot solution is reached. The underlying assumption is that each decision-maker is doing its best given the decision of the other (and with quantity as the decisive variable).

Under the competitive solution, price and not quantity is the decisive variable. Under autonomous behavior they will continue to undercut each other.

The pre-emptive solution (also known as the Stackelberg model) occurs when firm 1, with knowledge of firm 2's reaction curve, chooses an output level and proclaims that this will not be modified regardless of what firm 2 does.

The threat solution is a strong case of stay-out pricing. Firm 1 proclaims that if the other firm enters the market at all, it will produce enough to drive prices down to zero. If the threat is taken seriously, firm 2 may as well stay out of the market.

The question is, which of these models gives the best description of the pricing process in duopoly (and oligopoly)?

Of course the models are based on such simplified assumptions that you cannot expect them to describe actual situations realistically.

We have previously stated that duopoly (or oligopoly) on a homogeneous market is a theoretical abstraction. As a consequence, the assumption of quantity as the decisive variable is unrealistic. In all the cases with which I am familiar, attention has been concentrated on price and not on output as such. But this implies that the Cournot solution only has a value as a mental exercise for economists and mathematicians. The unreality of the Cournot model was already pointed out by the French nineteenth century mathematician Joseph Bertrand.

The pre-emptive model is also constructed under the assumptions of very special quantity reactions and has no explanatory value.

But the first solution, collusion, is of great interest. It may be realized by a formal agreement. Or what is even more interesting, by some way of tacit understanding. This possibility will be dealt with in section 5 under the heading: The theory of joint profit maximization.

The purely competitive model is not without relevance even though it has to be modified when applied to a heterogeneous instead of a homogeneous market. Actual examples can be found in which prices on nearly homogeneous markets are competed down to 0. Thus, when two steamship companies carried the traffic on the Hudson River between New York City and Albany, it once happened that prices went down to 0. But such cases have the character of curiosities. On a heterogeneous market, prices will not necessarily be competed down to marginal costs. An equilibrium price level may be reached. We shall comment on that in subsection c.

Finally, we have the threat model. The problem of whether this model presents a realistic solution we shall postpone to chapter 9 under the heading: Predatory pricing.

These basic models are too simplified to be immediately adaptable. The problem is whether they can form the basis for the construction of more complicated but also more realistic models.

The basic models can be extended in different ways. The assumption of profit maximization can be replaced by other goals. Thus, in some duopoly situations, market share may be a more realistic assumption than profit.

An interesting example of an elaboration of a classic model is the analysis of Roy Radner.[51] He extends the basic Cournot model by weakening the assumption of strict rationality and instead assumes that each player is satisfied to get close to his or her best response to the other player's strategy. Although such an elaboration provides new details for the oligopoly theory, it does not basically alter the Cournot model. Its realism is therefore limited.

The elementary models assume autonomous behavior. But it is possible to construct models based on conjectural behavior. There are various models for price leadership that can be fairly realistic.

One factor that is decisive for which form price competition will take is the cross-elasticity of demand.

The demand for medicine is inelastic. This is partly due to the fact that it is the doctor who prescribes which product to use but it is the patient, with help from the government and insurance, who pays. A consequence is that the price cross-elasticities between competing products are low. Examples show that some products are sold at a price twice that of another almost identical product.

---

[51] Roy Radner, "Collusive behavior in non-cooperative epsilon-equilibria of oligopolists with long but finite lives", *Journal of Economic Theory*, No. 2, April 1980, pp. 136-154, 1980.

The price cross-elasticity between the two newspapers is probably fairly low but higher than for medicines. The two morning newspapers are different. Each has its own loyal subscribers and it could be possible to have different prices. However, between the luncheon papers, competition is so keen that neither of them would dare to charge a higher price than the competitor.

For the detergents, the cross-elasticities are still higher. Even a slight difference in price between competing brands within the same quality group will cause consumers to switch. Therefore, an active pricing policy by one competitor will invariably invoke retaliation by the others.

In existing models the duopolists act rationally. But as illustrated by the examples, the managers are not automatic mechanisms that behave rationally but human beings with more or less personal motives. It is only natural if the rivalry between two duopolists may be conceived as a personal fight.

The realization that present duopoly (and oligopoly) theory is not satisfactory has motivated a number of economists to develop more advanced models. Economics journals often publish articles on duopoly. Whether such models represent a positive contribution to the descriptive theory depends on the realism of the underlying assumptions. But often they have the character of extensions of the traditional simplified models with some extra specifications added. Many of these models are interesting examples of refined logical analysis, often expressed in mathematical terms. But no matter how sophisticated the analysis, if the assumptions have no relation to reality, the models are excellent as an intellectual exercise but are of minor interest for a descriptive theory.

Let me confine myself to one particular model that contains some interesting aspects. The model deals with the incumbent-entrant problem: the relationship between an existing seller and a newcomer.[52] Boyer & Moreaux prove by use of a simple example that, in an incumbent-entrant setting, there is a clear advantage of being an entrant when both firms use both quality and price as their strategic variables.

The example is constructed as a three-period model. In the first period, the incumbent chooses price and quantity; in the second period, the entrant chooses price and quantity; and in the third period, consumers buy. The model leads to the conclusion that it is more advantageous to be an entrant than an incumbent. Unfortunately, the assumptions are absolutely unrealistic. I have never observed a situation in which a duopolist chooses quantity as well as price. They practically al-

---

[52] The contributions to this theory are already numerous. The pioneering work was done by D. Kreps and J. Scheinkman, "Quantity precommitment and Bertrand competition yield Cournot outcomes", *Bell Journal of Economics*, 1983. A clear exposition is given by M. Boyer and M. Moreaux, "Being a leader or a follower: reflections on the distribution of roles in duopoly", *International Journal of Industrial Organization*, 1987. My comments also relate to a recent unpublished paper by P. Raimondis and M. Tvede: "On the advantage of being an entrant in a duopolistic market", Copenhagen 1992.

ways select their price. What is more important is that the conclusion is a logical consequence of the assumptions! Of course entrants have an advantage, as they can wait and see what their rivals choose. But in real life, incumbents will practically never play a passive role. They will react as soon as the entrant has appeared on the market. The model gives the false impression that the entrant may have an advantage. But in practice, the advantage is invariably with the existing firm, which is already established on the market.

Models based on unrealistic assumptions are worthless, although of some interest as mental exercise.

6.4 Oligopoly and game theory

Economists have developed a great number of oligopoly models, each of which attempts to explain certain phenomena. But one theory was intended at least from the beginning as a general theory of oligopoly: *game theory*. Therefore I shall discuss whether my impressions and experiences can be brought in harmony with game theory. A huge literature is available, and the theory has expanded into a great number of sophisticated models. Here we have to limit ourselves to the basic ideas in the elementary theory.

Following the usual pattern, I first discuss game theory as a descriptive theory and in section 6 discuss whether it is useful in a normative sense.

Oligopoly really can be considered a game. On an oligopolistic market there are elements of conflict and elements of parallelism of interests.

Following the tradition of game theory we shall confine ourselves to the simplest case: duopoly.

A simple model is one in which the goal of each duopolist is to maximize its market share. This is a zero-sum game, because what one wins the other loses. This game is of some interest to economic theory, because market share often is a relevant goal, and some markets have a stable size in which you can only increase your sales at the expense of others.

We shall, however, concentrate on another model in which the goal of each of the duopolists is the maximization of profit. This is a non-zero-sum game, because the joint profit is not a fixed sum. The gain of one player need not be equal to the losses of the other. The idea in the game is that the profit of each of them not only depends on their own price but also on the price choice of the rival. The model is static and based on the assumption that both prices are set simultaneously. Thus, none of the players can wait and see what the other does.

The idea of the game can be illustrated in the following simple table. It is simplified in the sense that it is assumed that each duopolist has only two alternative strategies: the price can be 8 or 10. Variable unit costs are assumed to be 7 for each of the players. The payoff table indicates price (p), sales = production (s) and profit (G).

Payoff table

		B's strategies			
		$p_B = 10$		$p_B = 8$	
A's strategies	$p_A = 10$	$m_A = 100$	$G_A = 300$	$m_A = 35$	$G_A = 105$
		$m_B = 110$	$G_B = 330$	$m_B = 200$	$G_B = 200$
			$G_T = 630$		$G_T = 305$
	$p_A = 8$	$m_A = 200$	$G_A = 200$	$m_A = 120$	$G_A = 120$
		$m_B = 35$	$G_B = 105$	$m_B = 160$	$G_B = 160$
			$G_T = 305$		$G_T = 280$

As the table is constructed, the worst that could happen to A would be that he sets a price of 10, but is undercut by B. Correspondingly, the worst that could happen to B was that he charged the price 10, but was undercut by A.

In the most elementary game theory it is assumed that both of them want to play it safe, that is, maximize their minimum payoff. If A chooses $p = 10$, the worst that can happen is that he only obtains 105. But if he sets $p = 8$, he is guaranteed a minimum profit of 120. Therefore, the best strategy will be to set the price at 8. B is expected to reason along similar lines. He will run a risk if his price is 10 and A undercuts him. Therefore he must have a preference for $p = 8$. He has the chance that $p_A = 10$ and he will hit the jackpot, and he is guaranteed earnings of at least 160. Therefore if both of them follow a "minimax" strategy, in other words choose the alternative that gives the highest minimum, the price will be 8. This is an equilibrium in the sense that neither party has any motive to change the choice.

This solution is paradoxical in the sense that, of all the alternatives, it is the one that gives the lowest joint profit (280). Both of them would be much better off if they dared to choose the price 10, as the joint profit would be more than doubled (630). Even though this is a constructed example, it gives an idea of the great difference between the best and the poorest solutions. How could these duopolists maximize their profits despite the structural incentives to price low? The natural solution is for the two rivals to make the price agreement that the price shall be 10. Thus, collusion looks like such an obvious alternative that it could be expected to be realized in most cases in which agreements can be made and enforced. I have already mentioned that, in all the cases of duopoly (or oligopoly) of which I know, there is some sort of contact between the rivals. This does not necessarily imply that they make a formal cartel agreement, because implicit arrangements can be just as effective and more legally acceptable. (In the next section we shall return to the question of whether it is possible for the players to realize the alternative that gives maximum joint profit.)

Is it a hypothetical possibility that the best solution can be achieved without collusion? It is in theory. Both of them should reason that the other must realize that, by choosing the price 8, the situation is locked; whereas a price of 10 offers the best chance. But the risk is that the other does not follow this line of reasoning. Hence in this static example, in which communication is not possible, it is unlikely that the maximum solution can be realized.

Let us take another example. Oligopolists in an industry have either formed a price cartel or have a tacit agreement not to compete on price. Each firm has two choices: to be loyal to the cartel or to chisel and openly or secretly give price concessions. It is in the mutual interest of all firms to resist the temptation to undercut, but each firm is motivated to be disloyal and chisel. And every firm may very well reason that another is likely to be disloyal, so therefore it might just as well do it itself. If everybody selects this strategy, the oligopolists are doomed to arrive at the joint minimum solution. But the maximum solution is not excluded. Each firm may resist the temptation to expand its sales by price-cutting and take the chance that all are loyal – knowing that any individual gain of being disloyal will be shortsighted.

In the example with tranquilizers, until firm B entered the market, the three existing firms were absolutely loyal to a tacit price agreement. It is likely that a contributing factor to this loyalty was that the possible gain by undercutting must be regarded as low. Thus, the temptation was not great.[53] Otherwise, if cross-elasticities are high, then there will always be a strong temptation to expand sales by lowering prices. Only the fear that such disloyalty will start a ruinous cut-throat competition may have a sufficiently moderating effect.

Can game theory contribute to the explanation of price behavior in oligopoly?

In my opinion, the contribution is very modest, and at least the theory cannot give the comprehensive theory of oligopolistic behavior that was hoped for. There are various reasons for this:

* In its elementary form the theory is static. The rivals set their prices simultaneously. But that is not the normal situation in practice. In our example, if A sets the price at 10 and B at 8, it will often – though not always – be possible for A to reduce its price immediately. Hence time-lags are important. If immediate retaliation is possible, it will dissuade a firm from an active strategy.

Submitting of tenders is a special situation in which the pricing is simultaneous. In its simplest form, the firm that gives the lowest bid gets the contract, and the payoff for all others is zero.

---

[53] For new entrants the situation is different. They start with a low market share and their loss from price-cutting is therefore trivial.

- In normal cases of oligopoly, the rivalry has existed for a considerable time and the rivals will often be able to guess each other's strategies. The firms in the detergent industry knew one another intimately and had, for example, a fairly correct impression of the others' financial situation. Nevertheless, the strategy of a rival sometimes came as a surprise.

- When tenders are submitted, the firms often know each other, because the same firms participate in the bidding. A typical situation is a municipality in which the same local firms are invited to give bids each time there is a call for tenders. Experience has shown that some firms are better than others at predicting the strategy of their rivals and therefore get the contracts more often.[54]

- We have previously mentioned that there normally will be some contact between the oligopolists. Even though this does not necessarily lead to collusion, it will at least imply that the most undesirable situations are avoided. In our numerical example, the realization of the minimax solution was based on the assumption that the rivals feared each other and had no form of contact.
  But even with a minimum of contact, chances are that they can arrive at a better solution.

- There will often be common sources of information and communication between the oligopolists. Thus, for example, in the detergent industry, the medicine industry, the department stores and the publishing houses, there is an organized exchange of monthly sales figures.

The explanatory value of game theory is not great. But its predictive value is even more limited. One of the reasons for this is that the players are not automatic mechanisms but human beings. It is easy to imagine two identical situations in which the players act entirely different in the two cases.

But a careful study of the behavior of the rivals will often give a good foundation for prediction. When it is clarified which strategy each of the

---

[54] In Denmark, many municipalities previously practiced a system with regulation of the submitted bids. The reason was the sad experience that it often turned out that the lowest bidder was not able to fulfill the contract but went broke before the work was finished. Hence, there could be a certain skepticism towards a bid that looked too low. The regulation took different forms. One method was that the average of all bids was calculated. Bids lower than 15% of the average were cancelled. More sophisticated methods of regulation were also applied. Here was a field where game theory could be applied. Detailed studies have proved that some firms were better than others in this guessing game. But the studies also disclosed that cheating often occurred. One bidder could, for example, ask one of his colleagues to offer an extraordinarily high price, and he would know that the average price would be higher than normal.

oligopolists follow, it may be possible to predict the most likely outcome in a certain situation.

When we have been critical towards game theory, it must be underlined that this is in its elementary static form. If the theory is to be applicable, it has to be based on more realistic assumptions. Much work has been done already and more is in progress.[55] As an illustration, take the possibilities of using game theory for bidding at auctions: "Most analysis of competitive bidding situations are based on the assumption that each auction can be treated in isolation."[56] This assumption may be unrealistic for various reasons.

There may be several auctions simultaneously. Thus, when the U.S. Department of the Interior auctions drilling rights for oil, it may offer many tracts for sale simultaneously. More important is the fact that each auction has to be seen as a part of a dynamic process. According to Migrom & Weber:

> "The analysis that we have offered seems reasonable when the bidders do not know each other and do not expect to meet again, but it is less reasonable, for example, as a model of auctions for timber rights on federal land, when the bidders (owners of lumber mills) are members of a trade association and bid repeatedly against each other."

Thus, "much remains to be done in the theory of auctions". It is up to the future to develop a dynamic game theory that may help in explaining different types of the process of pricing. And it still has to be seen whether good knowledge of the theory improves players' chances of winning.

6.5 The theory of joint profit maximization

One aspect of game theory was the possibility of realizing the situation that maximizes joint profit. This could be done by way of collusion, but the interplay between the oligopolists can give the same result. But only as the consequence of conjectural behavior.

Originally the idea of joint profit maximization was introduced independent of game theory.[57] The theory in itself is intuitively convincing. According to Scherer[58]:

> "Any realistic theory of oligopoly must take as a point of departure

---

[55] See the articles in Ariel Rubinstein, *Game theory in economics*, 1990.

[56] Paul R. Migrom and Robert J. Weber, "A theory of auctions and competitive bidding", *Econometrica*, 1982. Reprinted in A. Rubinstein, *Game theory in economics*.

[57] This theory is presented clearly in William Fellner, *Competition among the few*, 1949.

[58] Quoted from F.M. Scherer, *Industrial pricing policies*, Chicago, p. 29.

the fact that when market concentration is high, the pricing decisions of sellers are interdependent, and the firms involved can scarcely avoid recognizing their mutual interdependence. If they are at all perceptive, the managers of oligopolistic firms will recognize too that profits will be higher when cooperative policies are pursued than when each firm looks only after its own self-interest. As a result, we should expect oligopolistic industries to exhibit a tendency towards the maximization of collective profits, approximating the pricing behavior associated with pure monopoly. Still, coordination of pricing policies to maximize joint profits is not easy."

A variant of the theory is that a group of firms may attempt to maximize their joint profit. There is rivalry within the group, but at the same time there are certain mutual interests. The group may consist of a number of small competitors, as is the case in the detergent industry. There definitely is rivalry between the big firms, but there is also a feeling of coherence against the small competitors. Or the group may be the retailers in a little town, who have a mutual interest in strengthening the attractiveness of their location. Thus, different forms of behavior can be observed for gasoline stations. In some localities the stations compete almost autonomously. But in other places their behavior is more sophisticated. They realize that they cannot win market share from each other, because any strong activity will immediately provoke retaliation from the others. So they understand that, if they are to expand sales, it has to be from other localities.

Is the theory of joint profit maximization realistic in cases of oligopoly?
    The difficulty in verifying the theory is obvious, as there is no conclusive proof. The actual profit of each oligopolist can be determined but not the hypothetical joint maximum. To this must be added the "normal" uncertainties such as whether it is the short- or long-term joint maximum that is relevant. The only way forward is through careful observation of the behavior of oligopolists to judge whether their policy is consistent with the idea of maximum joint profit. Therefore I shall try to judge whether my observations and experiences can be interpreted in such a way that they can be brought in agreement with the theory. But as each case is only an example and the number of examples limited, the conclusions can only be tentative.

In the case of the two *newspapers*, when one of them stated that it did not need a price increase, it prevented any increase in price.
    Is it likely that an increase in price at that time would have improved the financial situation for both newspapers?
    In my mind there is no doubt that the answer is yes. Thus, we have a situation in which the price behavior cannot be characterized as joint profit maximization. There are various reasons for that. One is that increasing circulation and not profit is the primary goal. Profit is necess-

ary in order to survive, but in day-to-day decisions, maximum circulation plays a greater role.

But that is not the only explanation. Through time the two newspapers have cooperated in certain situations, but not in others. There have been cases in which they have not been able to agree on a common course – even though it would be beneficial to both parties. It is my personal impression that if a certain mutual action could increase profit for both newspapers, but that 75% of the gain would go to number 1 and 25% to number 2, number 2 would find a number of excuses for not entering the project.[59] It is true that number 2 will gain, but it will be reluctant to accept if number 1 gains more. In the actual case a likely contributing motive for the newspaper that rejected the proposal of a price increase was simple retaliation for the previous situation when the other newspaper refused to cooperate.

In the *detergent* industry, it is possible through time to find examples of mutual considerations between the oligopolists, and it is evident that they have certain common interests in relation to the low-cost brands. But it is difficult to consider their behavior as a sort of joint profit maximization, because they use more energy in competing against each other. The action of Green in 1982 is a clear deviation from any desire for joint maximization.

Some of the observations in the *medicine* industry could fit into a theory of joint profit maximization. In both of the illustrated cases, the behavior of the firms before B entered the market was as one could expect if the aim was joint profit maximization. Thus, if company B had never existed, a tendency toward joint profit maximization was a hypothetical possibility.

But we cannot know whether it really was. If the goal was joint short-term profit maximization, prices should probably have been higher as a consequence of extremely low price elasticity. And if the goal was joint long-term profit maximization, prices should have been lower to reduce the incentive for B to introduce its inexpensive products on the market.

All of the examples until now have been what could be termed single-product oligopoly. Even though all of the firms are multi-product companies, we have concentrated on one particular product. As an example of multi-product oligopoly let us choose the *department stores* in Copenhagen. There were three stores besides numerous smaller stores, so that the competitive situation had some of the characteristics of oligopoly.[60] Their mutual relations were a peculiar mixture of cooperation and com-

[59] The solution that it may pay off for the former to bribe the other into accepting is purely theoretical.

[60] The situation has now changed, as two of the stores have merged. Our treatment only refers to the period when there were three independent stores and the situation could be characterized as oligopoly.

petition, but with emphasis on competition. They competed fiercely but occasionally demonstrated that they were able to cooperate. Sometimes they exchanged relevant information; at other times all lines of communication were cut. What is relevant is that there existed an invisible and vague borderline between them. One of the stores (I) was a high-quality and relatively expensive store. The biggest one (M) was trying to combine quality and price. The last one (D) was well-known for its low prices and had the image of being the store for the entire family. And now we have the dilemma. It was to their mutual advantage to hold these borderlines, but to each of them there would always be the temptations to expand beyond the borders. Thus, in 1982 M introduced a more active price policy, which by D was considered as a challenge and a violation of the tacit understandings. It responded immediately by a price reduction of 25% on all ladies wear. The success was overwhelming, and sales doubled within a month. But the main purpose was to let the two competitors know that any attempt to obtain a low price profile would immediately provoke countermeasures.

It is correct that the three department stores felt that they formed a special group and that they had common interests in certain relations. But there was not the feeling of coherence that would be necessary for real attempts to realize a form of joint profit maximization.

Because one cannot prove anything, only vague conclusions can be drawn.

The very fact that there practically always is some form of contact between the oligopolists is an argument that joint profit maximization may be a reality. There is a mutual understanding of being in the same boat and of having some common interests. But such attitudes can better be explained by a desire to avoid ruinous competition than as a systematic tendency towards a joint maximum. There will nearly always be a conflict between shortsighted self-interest and mutual understanding. For an outsider – and even for an insider – it will normally be difficult to say beforehand whether self-interest will prevail over group coherence in a given situation.[61] The predictive value of the theory is therefore limited.

The hypothesis may be ventured that full cost pricing provides better opportunities for realizing joint profit maximization than does a marginal approach. As said previously, general adherence to a full cost philosophy may function as a form of collusion. The same may be true if specific rules of thumb are generally accepted. If full costing dominates a trade, price competition will be reduced, which may give room for joint profit. A generally accepted use of rules of thumb may have the same effect. Thus, the behavior of goldsmiths may be interpreted as being in harmony with joint profit maximization. The goldsmiths themselves

---

[61] It has sometimes been said that it is difficult to imagine the existence of explicit or tacit collusion without some pooling of revenues. See Don Patinkin, "Multi-plant firms, cartels and imperfect competition", *Quarterly Journal of Economics*, 1947. This point of view is not in agreement with my observations. Pooling agreements are rare.

would rather use the phrase that they want to avoid the ruinous competition that they fear would be a result of marginal reasoning.[62]

The situation is less clear with a system of flexible full cost, but cost considerations may still prevent keen price competition.

The following factors are decisive for whether competition on price can be neutralized:

- When overall income is low, the need for cooperation is high. But simultaneously the temptation to cut prices is higher. If that is the only way you can save yourself, you forget about group coherence.

- The chances are better in pure oligopoly than in a situation including small competitors.

- The chances are better if the barriers to entry are high. It is easier to create mutual understanding if the risk of new entrants does not exist.

- The lower the price cross-elasticities, the better the chances. Compare the medicine and detergent industries. The chances for neutralizing price competition is higher for medicine than for detergents. This is somewhat of a paradox. The very fact that price is so important for detergents makes it urgent to obtain a mutual understanding, but it is so much more difficult to obtain.

6.6 Oligopoly theory as a normative theory

After we have discussed the appropriateness of oligopoly theory as a descriptive theory, the next question is whether it is useful in a normative way. To what extent have I been able to benefit from a knowledge of oligopoly theory when serving as a board member or acting as an adviser?

Some theories, such as the Cournot model, give a fairly definite solution but are just as useless in a normative as in a descriptive way. Other theories do not give a precise answer as to what can be done in a specific situation. They only enumerate different possibilities. But that is exactly what management needs. Without the framework of a theory, management will often be confused, especially when an unexpected situation arises. It may not be able to consistently analyze all relevant possibilities but will concentrate on one more or less arbitrary alternative. A typical situation is that a competitor, without warning, reduces the price on an important item. Management is tempted to react in panic and cut prices – which may be correct in certain situations but not necessarily all.

The theory seems to be more helpful in duopoly than if there is more

[62] Chapter 5 footnote 7 provides an example of the (buying) price policy of some goldsmiths. This example may very well be interpreted as an attempt to realize joint profit maximization for a specific group.

than one competitor. With more rivals, the interplay between the competitors and the number of combinations is so great that it may be difficult to give clear advice. Often you have to limit yourself to enumerating a few strategic alternatives. But in cases of duopoly, chances for a direct application of the theory are greater. Even the very simple models may offer some help.

But the basic problem is whether you can form an opinion of your rivals' reactions. Oligopolists may have known each other for years and have formed ideas of their normal way of behavior. But you can never be sure and surprises occur. Many managers have underlined the uncertainty connected with decisions in oligopoly. For example, Mr. Coggin, who is responsible for pricing at Delta Airlines, said (in *The Wall Street Journal*, August 24, 1984): "It's like a nonstop poker game with the same few players. The more you get to know each other, the more complicated it gets."

Another method to estimate what your opponents will do is to work under the assumption that they will behave in the most rational way. But this expression can be interpreted in many different ways, unless you are perfectly sure of what their goal is. They may adhere to a shortsighted selfish policy, they may desire to obtain a mutual understanding, their goal may be to increase their market share and so on.

A special situation is when you have no former experiences to build upon. For example, this may be the case if you establish yourself on a new market.

An interesting example is a big Danish company that always had enjoyed a monopoly position, being the only company authorized to operate within its field. In 1990 the government expressed its will to obtain competition by creating a duopoly situation by granting a license to one (and only one) more company. The existing company knew in due time that the rival would be a financially strong competitor. Management was seriously in doubt what to do, as it had no experience with a competitive market.

The main points in the strategy, which was worked out beforehand, were the following:

- It was not considered possible to compete the new firm out of the market. Even if it were possible, the government would grant a license to a third firm.

- It was agreed that the rival firm should be contacted as soon as possible. No formal cartel agreement would be proposed, but it was desirable to obtain a gentleman's agreement. As the existing firm was in a strong position, it was expected that the newcomer would be more than willing to establish a form of mutual understanding.

- Even before the new firm had started operations, it should be informed about the strategy of the existing firm. Thus, it was underlined that any price cut below existing prices would immediately be followed by similar price reductions.

- Furthermore, all different lines of action open to the rival were analyzed. And for each alternative it was decided beforehand which strategy to choose.[63]

Finally, we have the question of whether game theory can be used in a normative way. I have not been able to use the theory. It may be helpful in the sense that it compels you to clarify possible strategic alternatives, but you do not necessarily need to formulate it in terms of game theory. The reason I have never been able to use game theory is that it is never possible to give even approximate numerical values to the different alternatives.

6.7 *Pricing under monopolistic competition*

The traditional theory of monopolistic competition is based on the following assumptions:[64]

- There are many sellers and buyers on the market.

- The products of the sellers are differentiated, but close substitutes to each other.

- There is free entry to and exit from the market.

- The goal of each firm is profit maximization (either in the short term or the long term).

- Each firm knows its demand and cost curves

Based on these assumptions, the theory formulates an equilibrium model based on the extra assumption that each firm behaves autonomously. It is supposed to reason in a marginal way that it is advantageous to cut prices as long as marginal revenue is higher than marginal costs. When marginal revenue equals marginal cost, equilibrium is obtained.

The interplay between the firms is less sophisticated than in oligopoly. Each firm simply takes the rivals' prices as given and will undercut if it seems to pay off. This basic theory is further developed into different types of price behavior. It will carry us too far to describe and analyze all different aspects of monopolistic competition. We shall limit ourselves to the elementary model and ask the usual questions of whether

---

[63] The competing firm has been started. The planned strategy has been successful, and cut-throat competition has been avoided.

[64] As originally formulated by E. Chamberlin, *Theory of monopolistic competition*, 1933.

it is acceptable as a descriptive and/or a normative theory. The condition is that all of the firms behave rationally. But can we rely on this?

Retailing is often used as an example of monopolistic competition. Instead of dealing with retailing in general, I have selected one typical situation.

In Kalundborg, a Danish provincial town of 20,000 inhabitants, there were, until 1983, 4 supermarkets and 7 grocers in the downtown district and 10 grocers in the residential areas. In addition, there were a number of specialist shops such as butchers, several bakeries, a fish market and a number of small grocers in the neighboring villages. There was competition on price, and the supermarkets were especially active on price. Many small shops had given up in the years up to 1983. A period of relative peace was broken in 1983 with the opening of a discount store affiliated with a nationwide chain. In 1984 one more discount store belonging to another chain was opened.

What were the effects of the discount store(s) on the existing retailers? And how did they react to the price challenge?[65]

Reaction was slow in coming. The downtown grocers felt an effect immediately, but the grocers in the residential districts were almost unaffected. The supermarkets initially noticed hardly any effect. After one year, one of the supermarkets discovered that it had lost 1.5-2% of its turnover to the discount stores. As time went on, all the supermarkets made the observation that there was an alarming decline in the sales of products such as sugar, detergent, toilet paper, cereal and other typical discount products.[66] They also observed that the average sale per customer had declined.

It became apparent that customers bought some products in the discount store and others in the supermarket. The supermarkets reacted by increasing their service and sales efforts after cutting the prices on the discount products. In some instances the discounting was so deep that a selected number of products were sold below the purchase price. As a result, the average gross margin in the supermarkets declined after 1983.

Initially the grocers were unaffected by the discount stores, as they had little effect on the grocers' trade. This early passive stance was inappropriate, as the supermarkets' active policy severely impacted the grocers.

Our main interest is connected with the reactions on price. Let us choose one particular product to illustrate what happened. Grocers

[65] The information originates from a study undertaken by J. Vesterholt and myself.

[66] In another town, a detailed study was made of the effects upon a big supermarket of a discount store placed next door to the supermarket. The study showed a radical decline in the sales of some typical discount goods, but a general increase in turnover. The low prices of the discounter attracted customers to the area, but as it had a limited assortment it also attracted customers to the supermarket. The net effect of the discount store on the supermarket was slightly positive.

purchased *sugar* at DKK 23.50 per kilogram. Quantity discounts were not available. As competition was already high on sugar, the margin had been squeezed so that the normal retail price was about DKK 27.[67] The discount stores sold sugar for DKK 18.95!

The reactions of the grocers varied. In some cases the grocers simply refused to act: "The profit margin is already low. I do not want to sell at a loss, so I am going to maintain my price." Some of these grocers did not survive, particularly the ones who were in the same immediate locality as the discount stores.

There are other examples in which the grocers met the challenge. The village grocers got tired of hearing remarks as: "You ask DKK 27 for sugar and I can buy it for DKK 19 in town. You must make an enormous profit on sugar."

So they cut their prices to the discount level. They were more likely to stay in business longer than the first type – but had a difficult time.

A third group reacted in a different way. They felt that both extremes were poor solutions. The direct loss on sugar could not be compensated for by increased sales of more remunerative products, yet they could not live with too wide a price difference.

It was evident that most of the retailers had no clear idea of what would be their best strategy. What would be the consequence of a normative theory?

The theory states that the discount price must be taken as given, and the aim must be to find the optimum price differential to this price.

This differential depends on two factors. The first is geography.

This is especially important for the grocers in the neighboring villages:

- The farther the distance from the discount store, the higher the price differential could be.

- Old people were more loyal to their grocer than young people. Thus, a grocer in a village with a population of an average high age could live with a relatively wide price differential.

- In a village in which many of the residents commute into town, the price differential could not be as high.

The other factor is the dispersal of consumer preferences. If all customers are of the same type, for example, all highly price-conscious, the grocers have only the choice to match competition or drop the product. However, there may be differences among the customers; some may prefer high quality irrespective of price and others remain extremely price-conscious. The discount stores cater to the price-conscious part of

---

[67] In bakeries the price was about DKK 30 and in a special shop that was open at night the price was even higher.

the market; the other retailers may target other consumers by choosing a strategy of relatively high prices combined with superior service and quality. It is obvious that this is not a general solution, but it is the rational strategy for the few. This is clearly illustrated in the aforementioned town. Most of the butchers tried to compete on price and went out of business. One of them located next to the first discount store emphasized high quality, specialities and high service. He not only survived but noticed a substantial increase in turnover. A fish market offers another example.

In oligopoly the rivals react quickly, sometimes immediately. Under monopolistic competition, it takes time before the effect of the rivals' actions is registered and still more before the strategy can be selected.

This can be illustrated by the price policy of gasoline stations. When discount gasoline stations first appeared in Denmark, it took about 5 years before the established companies found the proper answer. In the beginning they ignored the few discount stations. And then when the threat became too obvious they reacted in panic by lowering prices in general. They finally realized that the best strategy was local price discrimination where the discounters were active.

7. Multi-product Pricing

7.1 Joint production

Practically all firms produce and sell a range of products. Multi-product firms can be divided into two categories: joint production in which, for technical reasons, it is not possible to produce one product without simultaneously obtaining other products. To the other category belong the majority of cases, in which the products are alternative in the sense that the production of any product can be discontinued at any time.

In all cases in which two or more products are made from the same common raw material, you have joint production. Examples are plentiful: fuel oil and gasoline, meat and hides, liquid oxygen and nitrogen, timber and saw dust.

Over time, there has been a tendency for joint production to play a greater and greater role, as it becomes more common for products that were previously treated as waste to be converted into saleable goods.

Joint production can be divided into two categories depending on whether the relationship between the output of the different products is technically fixed or can be varied. Often there is flexibility within certain limits only. In oil refineries, variable proportions in the output can be obtained through changes in the production process. You can find many examples of joint production with variable proportions within agriculture. You may, for example, vary the quantities of milk and meat by varying the age of slaughtering or the breed of cows.

The relative importance of joint products often changes over time. An example is the petroleum industry, in which manufacturing techniques have been evolving. In the refining process, crude petroleum kerosene was originally the major product and gasoline and lubricants were less important. The demand for gasoline and lubricants gradually increased, and kerosene became a minor product. This development has stimulated technical innovation so that now a larger volume of the high-demand products can be produced.

Let us start with a presentation of the traditional theory for determination of optimum price and output of joint products in fixed proportions. This is illustrated in Fig. 7.1: A is the main product, and B has the character of a byproduct.

D_A and D_B indicate the two demand curves and MR_A and MR_B the corresponding marginal revenue curves. As the two products are produced jointly they can be regarded as a product package. If one more unit is produced, the net gain in revenue is the marginal revenue from product A plus the marginal revenue from B. The total marginal revenue function MR_T is found by vertical addition of the individual

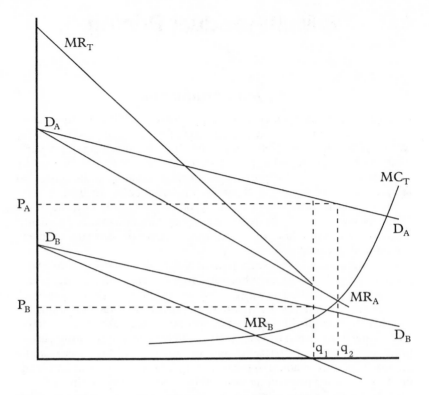

*Figure 7.1 Optimum price and output determination of joint products pro-
duced in fixed proportions*

revenue curves. The intersection with the marginal cost function determines the optimum output of the product package and the optimum
prices of each of the two products. As Fig. 7.1 is constructed, MR_B is
negative above the production level q_1. The optimum output is q_2, but it
will only pay to bring q_1 units of B on the market, which can be sold at
the price p_B.

We have assumed that there is only one marginal cost function relevant to the product package. But in addition to this joint marginal cost
curve, there are normally separate marginal cost curves for each product. Joint costs are incurred before the products are separated in the
production process.

For example, the purchase price for a chicken and the cost of slaughtering are joint costs for chicken meat, feathers, blood and so on. But
there will be separate costs for each product after they are technically
separated. Thus, feathers have to be washed and cleaned and put into
bags before that particular product can be sold.

The separate marginal costs curves should be added to MC_T, but
only for the output that is actually brought to market. Thus, the separate

costs for B are irrelevant in the output range p_1 to p_2. The marginal costs of B may be so high that it simply does not pay to sell the product.

According to theory, any allocation of the joint costs is arbitrary and even misleading. But the separate marginal costs of each product have to be determined. Such a determination is not always easy when there is flexibility in the production mix. Consider an oil refinery that wants to determine the marginal cost for a special oil with a low sulfur content. The desired result can be obtained in a number of ways. In an existing refinery the oil can be produced by mixing different raw oils and, in principle, it is possible to determine which mix will provide the lowest cost. If desulfurizing is obtained by varying the mix, then further reduction in the sulfur content will cause progressive costs. An alternative would be to construct a special installation for desulfurization, which would create a different cost structure. In the last alternative, the separate costs may have the character of fixed costs. If an entirely new desulfurization plant is built, the cost of producing low-sulfur oil is likely to be lower. Thus, the marginal cost of each specific technique is an ambiguous concept. There is an entire range of marginal costs, each corresponding to a particular method of production used.

In principle, you first have to determine the optimum product mix.

This requires knowledge of the separate demand curves, the production constraints and the cost consequences of varying the production mix. The solution is determined simultaneously in one mathematical system of equations. Modern computer techniques have permitted great progress in this field, and many firms are now using advanced systems. Such methods have been well used in the oil industry. However, not all firms have access to such computer technology nor do they have the relevant information.

Most decisions on production and price are taken by more primitive methods. The problems have always been a mystery to the producers, and rules of thumb have been – and to some extent still are – widely used. When one product clearly is the main product, it has been a common practice to allocate all joint costs to this product and calculate total unit costs. For the byproducts, price is determined by demand only. You simply sell them for what you can get. And if you cannot obtain a positive price, they are regarded as waste and discarded.

If more products are of about the same value, this method cannot be used. Some companies have experimented with homemade methods of allocating all costs to the products – but have often given them up again as hopeless. It is my impression that few firms nowadays attempt to allocate costs. But there are still motives for the allocation of costs. One is the importance many firms attach to internal accounting and control. Another motive is the regard to public controlling authorities. How can a price control board exercise its obligations if there are no calculations? And in an antitrust case in which a firm is accused of predatory business practices, the accounts may undergo judicial examination. The problems are illustrated by the following case in the United States.[68] Northeastern Telephone Company accused another telephone company of predatory pricing by lowering the price of one product to drive rivals out of business while subsidizing the predatory practice with higher profits on other products. The statement of Circuit Judge Kaufman in the case is highly informative:

> "Northeastern's argument in favor of a fully distributed cost test is based on a misunderstanding of the economic notion of subsidization. Northeastern seems to believe that whenever a product's price fails to cover fully distributed costs, the enterprise must subsidize that product's revenues with revenues earned elsewhere. But when the price of an item exceeds the costs directly attributable to its production, that is, when price exceeds marginal or average variable costs, no subsidy is necessary. On the contrary, any surplus can be used to defray the firm's nonallocable expenses."

I have already indicated that the primitive and arbitrary methods of former generations gradually have been replaced by more correct methods.

Let us illustrate the application of the theory by one particular example: the poultry stations.

In addition to chicken meat, the main product, a number of extra products are generated: intestines, blood, bones, feathers, irregular pieces of meat and so on. Until a few decades ago, these products were simply treated as waste. If anybody was willing to pay for them they could have them. Thus, waste meat was sometimes sold to mink farmers; sometimes they could get it for free, if they collected it themselves. The remainder was thrown away – usually dumped in the nearest river.

Today the situation is different. Careful analyses are made for each product, including chicken meat itself. It is realized that demand for the main product is highly elastic, due to intensified international competition. In contrast, the demand for many byproducts is limited, but less elastic. Some of them can only be sold in the local market, where no competitors exist. For a few products, such as blood, it has not been possible to find a market.

Fig. 7.1 demonstrates the basic principle for determination of quantity and price. The application of this theory to chicken products is illustrated in Fig. 7.2.

A-A represents the demand curve for chicken meat and B-B for waste meat. Fig. 7.1 is constructed so that A-A indicates the demand per kilogram of chicken meat as a function of price. B-B indicates the demand for the amount of waste meat that corresponds to one kilogram of

---

[68] Northeastern Telephone Company v. American Telephone and Telegraph Company. 1981. The case is here quoted from Call & Holahan, *Microeconomics*, 2nd edition, p. 240.

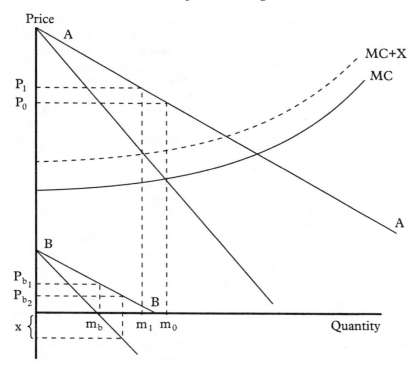

Fig. 7.2 Price and output of waste produkt and main product

chicken meat. Chicken is the main product and, as both products appear in the same production process, joint marginal cost is incurred. The optimum quantity of chicken meat is determined as m_0. The corresponding quantity of waste meat cannot be sold at a positive price. The theoretical solution is to sell m_b of waste meat and throw the quantity $m_0 - m_b$ away.

This solution meets difficulties today, because the environmental authorities do not allow the dumping of waste. The slaughterhouse has to get rid of this excess quantity, for example, by destruction, which costs money. Let us assume that the cost of disposal for each kilogram of chicken meat is x. This extra cost must somehow be covered. There has been great confusion over what the correct policy would be. The initial step, of course, was to protest to the official authorities, emphasizing that the Danish poultry industry would lose its competitiveness in the international market. As this argument made no impression, it was necessary to destroy the waste products that could not be sold.

A decision had to be made as what to do with these extra costs. Some of the arguments brought forward are interesting. There was a general consensus that, due to the competitive situation, these costs could not be defrayed by chicken meat. But somehow they had to be covered. The costs were caused by the byproducts and thus had to be included in the price for these. This is in agreement with the activity-based costing (ABC) system,[69] in which costs are allocated to the products that have caused them. But this argument was not accepted by the economists. They found that the correct solution is as indicated in Figure 7.2. The destruction cost, x, must be added to the ordinary marginal cost, because if one more chicken is slaughtered there will be additional waste to dispose of. Thus, the new marginal cost curve is MC + x, which leads to an increase in the price of chicken meat from p_0 to p_1. For the waste product, the marginal cost is x, but it is negative because it is only paid if the product is not sold. Thus, the correct solution is to decrease the price on the byproduct from p_{b1} to p_{b2}.

Although this theoretical approach must be logically correct, it has been difficult to carry out in practice. One problem is that for most by-products, the quantity of waste at each poultry station is too small to permit a remunerative transformation of waste products into saleable goods. The solution has been to establish joint production facilities for a number of poultry stations. A problem is that the transportation of waste products over long distances is very costly. Nevertheless, these practical problems have been solved with such success that the income from the byproducts exceeds the income from chicken meat. This is due to the fact that price elasticity is so much higher on chicken meat. The greatest success has been the production of pet food from waste meat and intestines. The success has been so tremendous that the slaughter-houses could not survive without pet food, as the contribution margin of chicken meat gradually has become negative. The paradox is that it always would have been remunerative to manufacture pet food. But it was not until they were forced to that the poultry stations took the relevant initiative.

7.2 Multiple products

Practically all firms manufacture a range of products, even though it is not a technical necessity. There may be different kind of relations between the items of a multi-product plan:

- products that differ in size, such as shoes and dresses;

- products that differ in color, for example, the same dress in various colors;

- products in different qualities, for example, the same product in first, second and third quality;

- products that are differentiated in time, for example, early and late performances; and

---

[69] See chapter 2.

- products that are related in demand. Special cases are repair parts, extra accessories and the like.

In addition to this are all the cases in which several products simply are manufactured in the same plant. Thus, a manufacturer of cars may also produce airplanes. And an ordinary supermarket has a rich variety of goods not necessarily related to each other.

The theoretical principles for multi-product pricing are clear. First, marginal cost and marginal revenue must be determined for each product, then the cost and demand relations between the products are clarified and, finally, corrections are made to determine the overall optimum. This can easily be demonstrated in a textbook example using 2 or 3 products. But when there are hundreds and thousands of commodities you have to simplify your methods. In the future you may base your decisions on simulation models with numerous mathematical functions. But today less sophisticated decision rules are used. The business executive manufacturing 1000 different products needs a workable price formula. As mentioned in chapter 4, such formulas are often based on cost concepts and may be rules of thumb.

The most widely used procedures seem to be:[70]

- Prices are proportional to full cost. If the system is carried out systematically, the same net profit margin is added to all products.

- Prices are proportional to incremental costs. An example is cost plus pricing, when the base is incremental cost. This principle implies that the percentage contribution margin over incremental cost is the same for all products.

- Prices provide profit margins that are proportional to conversion cost. Conversion costs are the costs required to convert raw materials into finished products, and may approximately be determined as allocated full cost minus purchased materials.
  The philosophy behind this method is that conversion costs reflect the firm's contribution to social welfare. It is this social contribution that entitles the firm to remuneration.

- Prices are proportional to size. For example, eighth-page, quarter-page, half-page and full-page advertising rates in magazines are proportional to space. This is normally not the case.

- These systems are all based on cost. But the basis may instead be demand. Thus, the contribution margin may depend on the price elasticity of different market segments. Approximations include the ren-

---

[70] Joel Dean's analysis of product line pricing from 1951 is still one of the best introductions to the subject. Joel Dean, *Managerial economics*, Prentice-Hall, New York, 1951.

tals for a machine, in which the amount paid depends on the output of the machine. Or film rentals based on the number of movie-goers or gross profit of the cinemas.

- Prices may depend on the life cycle of the product. Thus, the price of a commodity is automatically reduced if it is not sold within 3 months.

The cost-oriented price formulas are often modified by demand considerations. Thus, rates for fraction-space advertising were originally proportional, but it soon became evident that this was not a rational system.

In selecting a pricing formula, there will be a tendency to choose the system that gives the best results, in other words, leads to price relations that do not conflict openly with demand considerations. As an example, we have previously mentioned the pricing of wine in restaurants.

So although most price formulas are based on cost, demand considerations are not necessarily absent.

There is one more point of view that plays a great role: ethical considerations. The motivation for a system of pricing based on conversion cost really is ethical. In chapter 6 we mentioned that existing firms often were reluctant to engage in local price discrimination. Part of the explanation is found in the fact that management was reluctant to abandon the principle that all customers should pay the same price.

Ethical considerations are of minor importance when the customer has freedom of choice within the product line. But when the customer has to buy a specific size, the problem is relevant.

Let us relate the problems of manufacturers of women's dresses. They have perfect knowledge of the distribution of sales for different sizes. They know that the sales of the extreme sizes, both large and small, are limited.

They can approach their pricing problems in different ways. One method is to base the price on the value of the product to the customer. This method would lead to uniform prices, irrespective of size.

If pricing is based on some form of cost, the picture is different. More material is used for the bigger sizes, but unless the material is costly, this is of minor significance. More important is the size of the production runs. The most common sizes are cheaper to produce than the very small and the very big ones. The cost of setting up a production run is fairly high, but when a run is in production, the marginal cost of one extra dress is basically the same irrespective of size. If manufacturers use a uniform price, the contribution margin of the extreme sizes will be low and even negative. Therefore, either they will not produce the extreme sizes or will charge a higher price. In the latter case, the manufacturers must justify price differences. This is easier for big than for small sizes, because the customer gets a little more when acquiring a sizable dress (although consumers may raise the criticism that they are being punished because they are over-sized). Their justification for the smaller sizes seems impossible. Consumers will never be able to understand why they should pay more for less material. Manufacturers may find it unethical to charge different prices, and the common practice is to charge uniform prices.

This pricing policy creates difficulties. Some small manufacturers have been able to save money by not producing extreme sizes and concentrating on the popular sizes, where they can undercut normal prices. This is the discount principle again, and the traditional manufacturers can be forced to use a more flexible price policy.

The problems are different in situations in which the buyer has a free choice. Here demand considerations play an important role. When dresses are sold in different qualities, prices could be proportional to cost. Most often prices increase at a degressive rate. But the reverse may be true.

The demand for top quality will often be inelastic, as consumers in this category have high income or are snobbish or ignorant. Thus, for jewelry, top quality is often priced extremely high. The price differences between qualities are often kept so small that it permits step-up pricing, in which customers are persuaded to buy one quality higher than they originally sought.

Another reason why demand considerations are so important is that the degree of competition may vary between the product categories. We have previously mentioned the pricing of repair parts. Repair parts can be separated into different groups:

- For some parts the customer can simply buy a standard product anywhere.

- Other parts the practical customer will be able to reproduce by using simple hand tools.

- Still other parts have to be the original brand.

These differences will normally be reflected in the price structure.

8. Transfer Pricing

8.1 Definition

A transfer price is defined as the price used for intra-firm sales of goods and services among the divisions of a business enterprise. The divisions may be located in the same country or in different countries, in which case it is called a multinational enterprise.

Determining transfer prices raises a number of well documented issues for domestic businesses. Special problems arise when the divisions are located in different countries, and the following observations relate exclusively to multinationals.

Cross-border merger and acquisition activity is becoming more and more common. Multinationals are playing an ever increasing role as suppliers of goods and services. Multinationals can be divided into different categories, from huge corporations with divisions all over the world to a single company taking over a foreign company. There are also differences in ownership. The parent company might be a sole owner, a majority shareholder or a minority shareholder. The overseas division may be at different stages of development. The division may simply be a sales arm established with the sole purpose of marketing the products of the parent company or it may have a production capability of its own. This is the typical situation for a hitherto independent firm that has been taken over.

The autonomy given foreign divisions varies. The independence of a pure sales division may be limited, but usually it will have the autonomy to set prices in the local market. There are also examples of foreign divisions acting largely independently of the parent company.

It is difficult to get a true impression of the degree of autonomy within a multinational corporation. The management of a local division will typically claim a fairly high degree of autonomy, whereas the central management of the parent company will concurrently express the opposite view.

Even for an insider, it is often difficult to get a clear picture of the autonomy of a local division, as there are not always distinct criteria to use as the basis for measurement. The division may believe that it can make certain decisions by itself, only to be interfered with by the head office. In many multinationals, as long as the division works well and transfers part of the annual profit to the parent company they are less likely to interfere.

In general, the local unit has a fairly high degree of autonomy, as it is universally acknowledged that qualified managers want to make their own decisions and they know their local market best. In many respects, the local division can therefore be regarded as a business unit itself with substantial autonomy. This tendency is often encouraged by the central organization.

One important criterion for the degree of autonomy is the extent to which the local unit is allowed to find suppliers other than the parent company. Usually, the business unit will place orders elsewhere if prices are lower than those of the parent company. For example, it is common practice for the national branch of a multinational oil corporation to buy supplies from the parent company, but they are not obligated to do so. The branch can make supplementary purchases elsewhere, and should the possibility of a favorable offer arise, it is free to accept.

A second important criterion is the way that transfer prices are determined for deliveries from the supplying to the buying unit. Sometimes prices are simply fixed by the parent company, but often prices are based on mutual agreement. The parent company may exert the main influence, but the local units are not relegated to a passive role and are sometimes very active. More than one international corporation has admitted that price negotiations with their subsidiaries are more cumbersome than with any outsider: "Local units are often extremely difficult to work with, and they argue in a way no outsider would ever dare."

In the following it is assumed that transfer prices are set according to mutual agreement.

Some researchers distinguish between various types of organizations. A useful distinction is that made by Eccles:[71]

> "In a *competitive organization*, there is little vertical integration between the various business units. The corporation consists of several relatively autonomous divisions encompassing all the necessary functions of a complete business with little inter-divisional dependence. In such organizations the decision-making responsibility is left to the business units."

> "In a *cooperative organization*, the various business units cooperate. Vertically integrated companies are usually of this nature. The business unit managers do not have as much autonomy as their counterparts in competitive organizations, and top management is likely to intervene directly in day-to-day operations."

> "*Collaborative organizations* combine the characteristics of competitive and cooperative organizations. Owing to the high degree of interdependence, cooperation is essential between the individual units, which also compete as individual profit centers. The inherent problem of transfer pricing is especially complex for collaborative organizations, and top management often encourages a competitive spirit. A competitive spirit may give peculiar results."

---

[71] Robert G. Eccles, "Control with fairness in transfer pricing", *Harvard Business Review*, 1983.

Thus, rather extraordinary transactions occurred in the Danish division of a multinational oil corporation. The parent company had negotiated a big contract in Sweden. The Danish division got news of this negotiation and ultimately secured the contract for itself by underselling the parent company. The goods were then delivered from the parent company to Denmark and shipped to Sweden. The same Danish division was at one time involved in keen price competition for a specific product with its Belgian sister division. At other times it gave direct support to sister companies experiencing difficulties. Such policies are complex and hard to fully understand. Therefore, considering a huge multinational corporation as one profit maximizing unit will give an entirely false impression.

Transfer pricing is not only relevant for the physical transfer of goods within a corporation because numerous variations exist involving some sort of payment. A complete list would include:

1. Services, such as guidance and consultancy. To solve a difficult problem, a local unit may need assistance from either corporate headquarters or from an outside expert. Many factors influence this decision. An important issue is whether headquarters will charge more or less than an outside expert. Alternatively, headquarters, on its own initiative, might send an expert of its own to one of its foreign divisions.

2. Contributions to the central organizations such as payment for research and development costs.

3. Contribution to the general overhead for the corporation such as:

   - royalties;

   - insurance premiums;

   - transportation costs;

   - various forms of fiscal payments, such as interest on loans granted from the parent company to a local division; and

   - forward-covering risk premiums.

8.2. Transfer pricing in theory and practice

The theoretical discussion of transfer pricing is relatively new. It was long ignored by economists as an issue of only secondary or purely formal interest, as it was generally accepted that transfer prices within a corporation could not pose a major problem. It was commonly held that, when a supplying unit delivered goods to a buying unit, the price would influence the registered profit of both units but leave the overall profit of the corporation totally unaffected.

Hirshleifer[72] proved that, in a perfectly competitive market with no transaction costs, the correct transfer price would be the marginal cost of the selling division. Hirshleifer proved that the shadow price would induce the most efficient allocation of the divisions of a multinational corporation so that global profits are maximized. He also proved that the shadow price determined in this way is equal to the arm's length transfer price that would be chosen if all divisions were run as profit centers and were required to maximize their individual profits.

Since then a number of authors have developed models of transfer pricing under constraining assumptions, so that current analysis can determine profit-maximizing transfer prices for given income taxes, tariffs and exchange rates.

However, the fundamental theory is still based on marginal cost or market price and has found its way to elementary textbooks on managerial economics. It is easy to demonstrate that a full cost price will lead to erroneous results. If the supplying division charges a price higher than the marginal cost, it might be possible for the buying division to exert its autonomy by securing supplies at a lower price from an outsider. This transaction would not maximize corporate profits. To quote one of the numerous textbooks on managerial economics:[73]

> "How could a company make such an error as to select the false optimum...in preference to the more profitable set of products. This error, which in practice must be fairly common, is a result of mixing two functions of accounting: the measurement of income and the guidance of decision."

Theory is clear on this issue: marginal cost is the correct expression for the transfer price. In practice, marginal cost is rarely used. Marginal cost might be debated but is normally rejected. Thus, a glaring gap exists between theory and practice. These findings correlate with the results of other researchers. According to a study in the United States, prices are determined for deliveries to foreign or domestic departments within the same corporations as follows:[74]

[72] Jack Hirshleifer, "On the economics of transfer pricing", Journal of Business, Vol. XXIX, July No. 3, 1956.

[73] Henry and Haynes, *Managerial economics*, 4th edition, Business Publications, Dallas, Texas, p. 483.

[74] Anita M. Benvignati, "An empirical investigation of international transfer price by U.S. manufacturing firms", in Rugman and Eden, *Multinationals and transfer pricing*, New York, 1985.

	Foreign	Domestic
Market price	24%	49%
Cost plus	57%	29%
Cost	14%	19%
Others	4%	2%

The groups are definitely not homogeneous.

Market price not only includes cases in which a normal market price exists but also situations in which the price is based on the price of competitors.

Cost plus indicates a form of full cost with the addition of a fixed profit margin. It is probable that most of the cases can be characterized as rigid full cost.

Cost can also be understood as full cost but with no profit margin added. Thus, it must be interpreted as zero profit cost.

A special variant of full cost includes a contribution to future investment in new machinery and research. It is meant as an approximation to replacement cost, even though the calculation may be more or less arbitrary.

Decades before economic theory took up the problems involved in setting transfer prices, practice struggled with it. Managers had to set prices and found little guidance in theory. Much effort has been expended, especially in United States corporations, on finding workable solutions. There is evidence of United States corporations having experimented for 20 years with different methods without reaching the ideal solution. In practice, the most common method can be characterized appropriately as muddling through. Prices have often been the result of a compromise, satisfying nobody and with no consistent method as a basis.

In all multinationals it is still regarded as a problem that has not yet found a satisfactory solution. To quote the manager of a Danish multinational corporation:

"When selling to our foreign departments we use some primitive, quasi-fair transfer prices which are definitely not optimum."

The different functions of transfer pricing

In order to understand the discrepancy between theory and practice, and why it has been so difficult for practice to find a workable solution, it is essential to understand the functions of transfer pricing. A transfer price may have not one but many different functions.

Theory is concerned with optimum *decision-making*. Sometimes it has been taken for granted that this is the only objective when transfer prices are set and, as such, the logic of the theory is self-supporting. A purchasing division will only want supplies from the outside if the price is lower than the marginal cost of the supplying division, and production will be allocated to the units that manufacture at the lowest marginal costs. This elegant theoretical solution suffers from all the difficulties connected with the concept of marginal cost.

Marginal cost may be a precise concept in a theoretical model, but not in practice. Imagine the following situation: a multinational corporation has its headquarters in New York and a division in Copenhagen. The Danish division must decide whether to ask for an expert to be sent over from New York or to employ a local management consultant. If the marginal cost of the American expert is lower than the salary of the local, the American will get the task. At issue is the marginal cost to the corporation of the American expert.

Travel and living expenses can be fairly estimated, but what about payment for the services of the American?

Marginal cost may vary from week to week. If the consultant is sitting in his office waiting for proper challenges, the marginal cost is nil. If he is in the middle of solving important problems, his marginal cost is likely to be extremely high. In practice these services will have one price and the availability is restricted.

Determination of resale prices

Local divisions are influenced by the prices paid to supplying divisions when they are determining customer prices. The price may be determined exclusively by the current market price, or more, likely is influenced by the level of the transfer price.

Profit center considerations

In practically all multinational corporations, profit centers are an important focus of attention. For central management, it is imperative to control all local divisions and measure their remunerativeness and efficiency. This information can be obtained in many ways, and accounting is used to register the profit of each division. Naturally, division managers do their utmost to ensure that their division shows as good a result as possible, and they know that the result is influenced by transfer prices. In some multinational corporations, it is a tradition to arrange an annual meeting with the managers of all divisions. At this meeting the annual results of each division are announced, and managers are keen to compare their own performance with that of their colleagues.

This profit control cannot be based on marginal cost. The unavoidable result would be the supplying departments showing a deficit, because their overhead is not covered, and all profit would be registered in the purchasing departments.

Therefore, the system is always based on some form of cost allocation. Economic theory acknowledges that such an allocation necessarily involves some degree of arbitrariness. In practice, prime attention is paid to the methods of allocation, and the division managers will fight allocation principles that they see as unfair. It may well be at the annual meeting that each person who represents a division's results will underline the arbitrariness and the fact that the figures are not to be taken literally. However, all these reservations are immediately forgotten and the psychological impact on the individual division managers of how their performance compares with that of others is enormous. This psychological effect is not limited to the managers. Employees feel embarrassed to be in a division that does not show a profit. The fear alone that their division may be shut down if it continues to register a deficit may be decisive.

The tax motive is evident to everybody, especially to politicians and tax authorities. By selecting appropriate transfer prices, it is always possible to register the profit in one of two countries where tax rates are lower. Multinationals, therefore, are often suspected of taking tax avoidance measures. This principle can be refined in different ways. For example, it is possible to let a certain delivery pass through a tax haven such as the Cayman Islands or Bermuda and determine the various prices in such a way that the entire profit is registered there. As this idea is obvious, the tax authorities in various countries, and especially in the United States, have issued regulations to prevent the most glaring abuses.

What is of interest here is the extent to which international corporations include such considerations in their price-setting and whether this affects pricing for other purposes.

Observation of the transfer pricing philosophy of a number of multinationals may lead to the following conclusions:[75]

1. The extent to which the multinationals apply tax avoidance depends on the control measures. For products with an established market price, the tax authorities have a basis for control. An example is the global oil market, but even here, control can never be complete, as this would require deep insight into the mechanism of the market. Only the most glaring cases of tax abuse can be detected. On highly specialized products, control is even more difficult.

2. For most international corporations, the majority of trade is between countries with limited differences in tax rates. Considering the risk of detection and the haggle with the authorities, the temptation to speculate in tax rates is limited.

3. The bigger the multinationals, the less they are inclined to speculate in tax rates. There are various reasons for this:

   • Decisions are taken by professional management interested in maximizing corporate profits but not in taking risks.

---

[75] This knowledge is primarily based on large and medium-sized multinationals and not on the smaller corporations.

- Big multinationals are extremely sensitive about their reputation and image. An accusation of tax evasion could be very embarrassing.

- When overall profit is already satisfactory, the extra margin that could be secured by tax speculation is often deemed not worth the risk.

- Big multinationals have many employees. Tax speculation would be known to a number of people inside the corporation, with the risk of leaks.

- Most important of all: what matters more than anything else to the corporation are profit center considerations in order to secure control of the operations of the entire corporation. The tax authorities might get a false impression, but invariably, management would also get a false picture of the corporation and would only have a fragmentary knowledge of the functioning of each division.

4. It is more common for small firms to speculate in tax rates. Sometimes the specific purpose of acquiring a foreign company or establishing a division in a tax haven is to minimize tax payments for reasons that are a consequence of what is said above:

- Taxes play a relatively greater role.

- The risk of losing the big picture is less.

- Fewer people know about the transactions.

- The risk of destroying its public image is less for a relatively unknown company.

This is not tantamount to saying that the big multinationals do not take tax aspects into consideration. Tax authorities now and then publish cases of tax evasion. Thus, in the United States it has sometimes been possible to show that multinationals operating in the United States, especially with a Japanese home base, show extremely low profits taxable by the United States authorities. But the companies may not take tax considerations for normal commodity transactions. The risk of being forced to comply is too high when there are much better methods. Payment for services, research and development costs and insurance premiums are a few examples. It is extremely difficult for any tax authority to judge whether payment from headquarters to a division for the performance of an expert is fair or not. It is commonly done for insurance premiums. A number of multinationals have established their own insurance companies in tax havens, especially in Bermuda, and these divisions are highly profitable.

Tariff considerations

If a value tariff on commodities is imposed in the country of the receiving division, this may favor low transfer prices to the importing country.

Government control

Multinationals may take into account the degree of control public authorities exert in various countries. Some multinationals admit that their knowledge of the zeal of the tax authorities is just as important as of the tax rates.

7.3 The practical solution

Determining appropriate transfer prices has caused problems for a long time, and many firms have tried to find feasible solutions. Many more or less sophisticated systems have been applied, usually with problematic results.

It is impossible for one price to simultaneously fulfill all the conflicting criteria. Often the actual transfer price is the result of a compromise between opposite points of view. But a compromise never provides the perfect solution.

An example illustrates this. In Denmark few firms manufacture farm machinery. Some years ago, one of the two major firms was acquired by a Norwegian corporation. After the takeover, an agreement on specialization was reached, so that certain parts were manufactured in Norway and others in Denmark. This specialization reduced overall costs. Subsequently, it was not as easy to reach an agreement on transfer prices. Finally a compromise was made. The prices were below normal full cost, but far higher than marginal costs.

In the beginning the system worked, but the unexpected happened. The workers in the Norwegian plant protested, their argument being that prices for deliveries from Norway to Denmark were fixed below normal cost, which they considered as a favor to the Danish division. The registered profit in the Norwegian division was lower, which weakened the bargaining position of the union. Management gave in to the argument of the workers and, as a result, prices were determined as full cost with the addition of a normal profit margin. The outcome of this was that the Danish division chose to buy some parts outside the corporation at a slightly lower price although there was idle capacity in the Norwegian plant.

7.4 The theoretical solution

As no single price can meet all requirements, the theoretical solution is clear. One must either select one purpose and ignore all others or apply a system of dual pricing. The latter solution, however, is not without its problems. Many corporations hesitate to adopt such a system, and the main reasons are:

1. A multi-price system may encounter administrative difficulties, but with modern computer techniques this problem is surmountable.

2. A number of people know of the existence of the system; it might be regarded as dubious to work with prices that vary on purpose, and the tax authorities are likely to be highly suspicious.

Nevertheless, from a theoretical viewpoint, a multiple system of pricing is the solution. One set of prices is the official prices, accepted by the public authorities, and applies in all official relations in, for example, the declarations of income. As a supplement to this, an additional set of prices might be used internally for other purposes. Decision-making could be based on marginal costs or the market price. A third system could be used for profit center purposes. This could be based on some sort of full cost pricing, but so that the managers of all divisions accept the cost allocation as fair and reasonable.

The idea is not only theoretical, as approximations are found in electronics companies in the United States.[76] The system can be constructed so that the buying unit buys the transferred goods at cost, and the selling unit is credited with the market price. The motive is to encourage the buying unit to keep its purchases within the corporation and if the cost is higher in, for example, the introductory phase of a new product, the receiving unit can be promised a special lower price. This is not an example of a constant causal pricing system, but rather of amendments to an existing system that avoids the worst mistakes.

A few examples of dual pricing can be found in Danish multinationals. One case involves a firm with divisions in a number of countries manufacturing different types of instruments. A dual pricing system is ideally suited, but management applies it in an awkward way. The cost price is used as the basis, as it is thought to be a reliable source to estimate the production costs of this particular product. An additional premium of 3% is added to cover the risk connected with variation in exchange rates. A substantial part of the competitive price remains unchanged. If the competition is high, the premium is low and might even be negative. If competition is low the premium is high. This is done out of respect for the tax authorities. However, management realizes that the system gives a distorted image of the division's relative profitability and their own abilities. An entirely different pricing system is therefore used within the corporation.

A second Danish example shows how practice gradually approaches theory. A dual price system is used for foreign divisions. Each unit pays a fixed annual amount to cover indirect costs to the parent company, and commodities are currently delivered at prices corresponding to the variable costs.

[76] Robert C. Eccles, "Control with fairness in transfer pricing", *Harvard Business Review*, 1983.

9. Price Discrimination

9.1 Conditions for price discrimination

Price discrimination is the practice of charging different prices to different buyers for the same product. True price discrimination requires that the products sold to different customers be identical. However, price discrimination is also used in a broader sense to include the practice of selling the same product in different markets at prices that are not in proportion to the differences in marginal cost.

In textbooks, price discrimination is often separated into three different types. With first-degree, or perfect discrimination, buyers are forced to pay the maximum price they are willing to pay. Thus, the perfect discriminator leaves no consumers' surplus. Second-degree discrimination is a crude approximation of perfect discrimination. The discriminators cannot obtain separate prices from each customer, but they can partition demand into blocks so that the price is different for each block of customers. Third-degree discrimination could also be called normal discrimination. The sellers are able to divide their customers into two or more groups characterized by different demand curves and with different elasticity. The highest price is charged to the groups with the lowest elasticity.

Four conditions must be fulfilled for a policy of price discrimination to work:

1. It must be possible to separate the buyers or groups of buyers.

2. There must be differences in price elasticities in the different buyers' demand functions.

3. Price competition must not hinder the discrimination. The result of this is that price discrimination is possible under a monopoly but not in a market with perfect competition.

4. Price discrimination must not be illegal. In most countries there are legal restrictions against price discrimination.

In the Scandinavian countries, a monopoly or price-directorate can declare an alleged case of discrimination illegal and, in practice, any type of price discrimination must be approved. In broad terms, firms have a fairly high level of knowledge of the conditions necessary for a specific system to be approved. In Denmark the normal conditions for the approval of a discount system are:

1. Discount rates are granted according to objective criteria.

2. Anyone fulfilling the requirements can obtain the discount.

3. The discount system is consistently carried through.

4. The system is openly publicized.

5. Discounts reflect cost savings, such as quantity discounts.

The result of this is that modifications must be made to the traditional theory of price discrimination so that only legal forms can be taken into consideration.

9.2 Price discrimination in practice

Price discrimination is common. It is superfluous to give a long list of examples. Of interest is whether price discrimination occurs when the conditions are not fulfilled or whether the conditions for price discrimination exist but are not utilized.

When price discrimination is unsuccessful, the most frequent cause is that the separation of the different markets has failed. For example, medical products are charged at different prices in different countries until the price differences are published in newspapers. It is then difficult to maintain the differentiation.

It is easy to demonstrate that, on occasion, price discrimination does not take place, even though the necessary conditions are fulfilled. If the theory were consistently observed in practice, price discrimination would take place in any situation in which there were buyers or groups of buyers with different price elasticities and in which some form of separation was possible. Numerous cases can be found in which this is not the case, and there is far from perfect agreement between theory and practice.

The major reason why many firms abstain from price discrimination is that they regard such a policy as unfair and want to avoid criticism.

When a form of price discrimination has become traditional, it is generally accepted. In the airline charter industry, price discrimination is sometimes carried to extremes. The prices for charter flights from Scandinavia to the Canary Islands differ from week to week. When you take your seat in the plane, there is a chance that your neighbor paid one third of what you paid because he risked flying as a standby passenger.

9.3 Predatory pricing

Predatory pricing is an attack in the form of a low price by a firm in a strong market position (usually a monopolist) on an entrant after the latter has actually opened business. If the low-price policy is chosen before the newcomer has become established, it is deterrent pricing. A theoretical possibility could be a nationwide chain of supermarkets. If a competitive supermarket is opened in a local market the chain may start a local price war to drive it out of the market again.

In recent years there has been a discussion among economists whether predatory pricing is a realistic possibility.[77] Many economists believe that it does not and cannot exist, except in cases of irrational psychopathic behavior. The main argument is as follows.[78] The costs of predation for the established firm in terms of losses, foregone profits and financial difficulties will normally be higher than the eventual loss of profit to the entrant. And it might be a more attractive alternative to absorb the new firm through merger. Other economists find that if certain conditions are fulfilled, predatory pricing may be a rational policy for a dominant firm.

Predatory pricing will normally be price discrimination. The existing firm may be a multi-market firm, and if a new entrant establishes itself on a local market, the firm may decide to reduce prices for that market only. And when the entrant has given up and left the market, prices will be increased to their normal level again. It is normally assumed that predatory pricing implies that prices are down to marginal cost or lower.

As a contribution to the discussion of whether predatory pricing is likely to exist or not, it is of interest to observe whether cases can be found on such a small market as Denmark.

It is difficult to find clear examples of predatory pricing. I know of cases in which such a policy has been contemplated but the idea was given up. And exactly for the reason stated above: fear that the costs would be higher for the aggressor than for the prey. But to this comes the fear that the attempted gain could not be obtained.

When the first of the small firms was established in the detergent industry, it was natural for the existing firms to contemplate a price war, as there was already excess capacity within the industry. But the idea was given up as unrealistic. The start of the firm was supported by a public development fund. The machinery could only be used for manufacturing detergent, and should the first owner be forced out of business, the equipment would be sold for almost nothing to the next owner, who would be likely to continue manufacturing.

A circumstance that plays a great role is the fear of losing goodwill. The existing firm is likely to be a big company, perhaps in a monopoly position. Public opinion and the local and national press will support the "little innocent newcomer" and the predator will be accused of exploiting monopoly power. The likelihood of a nationwide supermarket chain engaging in a local price war to stop a new entrant is close to nil, as this would immediately affect other local markets.

---

[77] An overview of the different arguments can be found in L. Phlips, *Predatory pricing*, Luxembourg, 1987.

[78] See J.S. McGee: "Predatory pricing revisited", *Journal of Law and Economics*, 1980.

For a monopolist, there are two types of newcomers. It may be a local firm, which theoretically could be forced to give up. But the sympathy is with the entrant and the loss in image too serious for the monopolist. Or the newcomer could be a foreign multinational corporation that wants to obtain a share of the Danish market. Here the sympathy may very well be with the Danish company, but the entrant is too strong to be competed out.

In addition, public authorities may have an influence, which may consist in direct or indirect support of the weaker part.

It is difficult to find clear examples of predatory pricing, but it is easier to find cases in which the big firm, by way of price-cutting, attempts to persuade a smaller firm to make its policy less aggressive.

For example, in the 1930s the Carlsberg breweries, which enjoyed a strong market position, tolerated a number of local breweries. But when a local brewery showed too much initiative by starting selling in the Copenhagen area, Carlsberg found this policy too aggressive. It began local price discrimination in the small brewery's own locality. It was not predatory pricing in the proper sense as Carlsberg had no intention of ruining the competitor, but only to make it give up the Copenhagen market. Furthermore the price was only lowered by a few percent (and far above marginal cost). But it did not take long for Carlsberg to realize its mistake. There was strong local support for the little brewery – but also in the rest of the country the sympathy was with the challenger! Since then Carlsberg has not tried any policy resembling predatory pricing.

9.4. Discount policy

A business will often have a formal list of prices, but different buyers or group of buyers can be granted a discount. There are businesses in which practically no one pays the official price, as everyone is granted some form of discount.

A discount is not necessarily price discrimination. If a discount corresponds exactly to a cost saving, then theoretically it is not price discrimination. As a general rule, a discount will contain an element of discrimination, and hence it is appropriate to treat all forms of discounting in this chapter.

Few firms have a consistent discount policy. Most often the policy can be characterized as muddling through. As one manager phrased it: "Our discounts depend on the size of the order and the impudence of the buyer."

Sometimes the main explanation for the accepted discount norms in an industry is tradition. For a new entrant to an industry, it seems natural to adopt the methods that are commonly used, without much speculation about whether they are rational or not. Quite often an analysis will prove that they are not.

I have often heard the comment from managers that they have looked in vain for clear guidelines on discount policy in textbooks of managerial economics. This makes me believe that a normative theory of discounting is needed.

The main emphasis of the following presentation is the normative aspects of the theory.

When business managers decide to develop a discounting system, they must first set out clear objectives. They may primarily be concerned with demand or cost or both. Considerations on the demand side may be for the consumers or the competitors – or both.

Consider the difference between a quantity discount and an annual bonus. The size of the quantity discount is determined by the size of the order, whereas the annual bonus depends on a customer's accumulated purchases over a year. In principle, a buyer can obtain a high annual bonus by submitting a great number of orders, even though many of the orders would be so small that they are of questionable value to the supplier. Therefore, the motive for a quantity discount is on the cost side, but for the annual bonus it is on the demand side. Suppliers in a highly competitive situation can use annual bonuses to enhance customer loyalty and encourage the concentration of purchasing through them. For a supplier in a strong monopolistic position, there is not a strong motive for giving annual bonuses.

After determining the level of competition, the next step is to analyze the operation of the business. If the discount system is based on cost considerations, it is necessary to determine the factors that influence the costs of the individual orders. If the system is based on demand considerations, it is important to gain insight into the probable reactions of customers to different discount systems and rates.

Often an analysis will show that an existing traditional arrangement is no longer appropriate – and maybe never has been.

The policy of a particular tobacco company offers a good illustration of how a traditional system was replaced by a much more efficient and rational arrangement. The company enjoys a strong, almost monopoly position, in the Danish market, so competitive considerations are of no relevance for developing a discounting system. The company's products are heavily taxed, and partly for this reason prices are fixed and controlled by the government. Traditionally, discounts were given on these prices to wholesalers and retailers and constituted their profit margins. The discount was somewhat higher to the wholesalers than to the retailers, permitting their existence. In addition, but of limited importance, a special discount was granted to all buyers who personally collected the products they bought. The obvious reason was that the company could save on transportation costs.

An analysis showed that the system was completely irrational. The process of concentration within retailing had resulted in a situation in which some of the retailers were much bigger than the smallest of the wholesalers, but it was the latter who received the highest discount. Furthermore, the costs of expedition were higher, not lower, when the retailers came themselves to fetch their goods. The personal visit of a retailer necessarily implied a certain amount of conversation and thus was more time-consuming than a normal order. The first consequence of the analysis was that retailers were no longer welcomed at the premises.

As demand considerations were insignificant, the analysis concentrated on the cost aspect. The main issue was to determine the factors that influenced the cost of an order. These costs were primarily labor costs. The most important factors investigated were:

1. The size of the order indicated by value.

2 The number of items in the order. An order might be for one article or more than 100 different articles.

3. The order may be for a standard package of 24 cartons or it may be for a fraction of a package such as 17 cartons.

The cost functions were determined by systematic experimentation over a year. Time studies were made to measure the time of receiving, collecting and shipping an order. A limited number of phantom orders were placed among the real orders. One hundred orders were constructed so that the value was approximately the same; one included one article only, another two, etc., and the last one was for 100 different articles. The cost as a function of the number of articles could be determined. The other partial cost functions were determined similarly.

The results were absolutely convincing – and somewhat surprising. The costs of delivering in fractions were not as high as anticipated. So the idea of a special charge for deliveries in fractions was abandoned. The dominant cost factor was not the size of the order (measured in value) but the number of items in an order. It was possible to construct a discount system based on the number of items and with perfect knowledge of the cost factors.

A second example of a discount system motivated by cost considerations is one used by a manufacturer of women's dresses. The manufacturer has great problems with production planning. Most of the production takes place half a year before the sales season. When orders arrive, the manufacturer can begin to forecast more accurately the number of each type of dress that must be made. Normally in the middle of the season, extra production runs are necessary for the most popular dresses. On average, each dress has to be manufactured three different times.

After analyzing what the average cost per dress would have been if they had had prior knowledge of the total sales, the manufacturer could offer a discount to all customers who placed their order before a certain date.

When the motive for discounting is based on demand considerations, it is important to form an idea of how consumers and competitors will react. In relation to the consumers, the purpose is to give low prices to some customers but not all. Consumer discounts may thus be positioned to prevent ordinary customers from utilizing the discount offer. An example is special introductory offers for new subscribers to newspapers and magazines. This method raises a number of problems. Experience shows that new subscribers often drop out again after a short period or are poor payers.

Granting discounts is often preferable to an open price cut, which can create difficulties when the price is increased again at a later date. A discount can be simply discontinued and the normal price put in its place. If a discount is announced as temporary, it may convince competitors not to retaliate with similar steps and start a price war.

9.5 Charging for extras

An extra charge can be regarded as a negative discount. Thus, you can have an official price, which is considered the normal price. For orders over a certain size a discount is granted, and an extra charge is imposed on small orders.

It is a natural part of a company's price policy to charge extra for all orders that cause special costs. This can often result in such a system being accepted grudgingly by customers because they do not immediately realize that they cause extra costs.

It may be a rational principle to inform the customers that they can have any special product they want and any individual demand can be fulfilled – on the condition that they are willing to pay the extra costs they cause. But the principle is difficult to carry through in practice because some customers protest violently against the extra charge. Therefore, in order not to ruin its image it may be a wiser solution for a business to inform the customer that the special request cannot be fulfilled.

Here we shall limit the discussion to typical forms of charges.

A special service charge can take different forms. It may be levied only on small orders, or it may be a fixed charge on any order combined with quantity discounts, so that the charge and discount balances for orders of a certain size, and larger ones obtain a net discount.

The introduction of service charges may meet resistance from customers. They may even make the remark: "Now you are charging just for submitting an order". But most experiences are positive.

An instructive example can be found in the Swedish textile industry. The biggest firms were pestered by a great number of small orders. One of the firms decided to introduce a system consisting of a service charge on any order plus quantity discounts for orders above a certain size.

The very idea of a service charge met with strong opposition from the retailers, and the retailers' organization distributed to its members labels with the text: "This order is submitted on the condition that no service charge has to be paid." Consequently, such orders could not be accepted.

The immediate result was a drastic reduction in the number of orders and a commensurate reduction in sales. Management was not stricken by panic and stood firm. After less than half a year the tide turned. Sales rose and average order size increased, with notable cost reductions as a result. The final outcome was an increase in profit.

I have personal experience with the introduction of service charges. The first case refers to the department stores in Copenhagen. To try to compete effectively against other similar types of retailing, they traditionally attached considerable importance to a high service level. All parcels were delivered free of charge to any customer within a fairly large region. Through time the system became more and more costly. After years of hesitation, management was finally persuaded to introduce a small charge for all parcels delivered to the customers. Management was highly nervous about the potential reaction of the customers, but there was hardly any. Customers simply took the packages with them more often.

Another example was the publishing houses, which finally accepted a proposal for the introduction of a service charge for books mailed directly to customers. The result was the same; there were hardly any negative reactions.

One common special requirement is a rush order. They are potentially costly because other orders have to wait and normal production planning is broken. The rationale is that a special charge covers the extra costs which are caused.

In this example, the customers cause the extra cost. There might be other situations in which they do not. Sometimes deliveries to a retailer have to be made within narrow time limits because of parking restrictions. Such a situation makes rational logistical planning difficult and causes higher costs. Even though the retailer finds it an injustice, it may be rational to levy an extra charge.

10. Vertical Relations

10.1 The basic theory

The vertical relations between firms are a mixture of cooperation and competition. For example in the traditional chain of producer – wholesaler – retailer – consumer, it is imperative that there be some form of cooperation. At the same time, however, a natural conflict of interest arises from the buyers' desire to obtain as low a price as possible and the seller's desire to obtain the converse. Vertical relations are not confined to the traditional chain. One wholesaler may sell to another wholesaler; one producer may work as a subcontractor for another producer and so on.

Parallel to the theories outlining a seller's pricing policy, there are theories that explain a buyer's purchasing price decision. The basic theory, called *monopsony pricing*, describes how a single buyer sets its purchase price towards a large number of suppliers. The profit-maximizing principle still determines the optimum for the buyer at the point at which marginal cost equals marginal revenue. This principle implies that the monopsonist can force the price down to the point at which each supplier is only able to cover its variable costs.

In the elementary model, the supplier has no options and must deliver to the monopsonist – or give up. But the basic model can be developed further by assuming that the supplier has other alternatives available. For example, farmers who deliver their products to a monopsonist could grow other products.

A market structure consisting of a monopoly against a monopsony is called *bilateral monopoly*. This structure may occur if the individual sellers form a single organization in order to enhance their negotiations with the monopsonist. When this happens, there is a fairly equal distribution of power between the two parties and therefore, in theory, there is not one optimum or equilibrium price. Instead, the price is determined by negotiation, with the outcome depending on such factors as the economic strength, negotiating skills and possible alternatives of the two parties.

Another type of market structure that has not attracted much theoretical interest is the *bilateral oligopoly*. This structure is characterized by a few firms with limited power on both the buying and selling sides. As with the bilateral monopoly, the price depends on the economic strength, negotiating skills and substitution options available to the various firms.

Our theme is whether such theories can be used to describe the pricing process in the real world. The pure monopsony theory is constructed as a normative theory. But can it also be used descriptively?

Monopsonistic pricing is synonymous with the exploitation of monopsonistic power, and history gives a number of cases when it has occurred. There are well known examples of the use of monopsony power in the United States, especially in the first decades of this century.

Such glaring exploitation of buying power is less realistic in most countries today, as governments typically intervene to protect the weaker parties. Therefore the relevant question is to what extent the theory of monopsonistic pricing is realistic in a modern, regulated economy.

In pure theory, it is assumed that one buyer controls 100% of the market. Such cases can be found. But often monopsonists have a market share of 80% or 90% and can still be dominant even though they do not have absolute power.

We have chosen to base our comparison of monopsony theory with reality on two Danish examples; one has 100% market share and the other has small competitors.

10.2 Examples of monopsony

The first example is the pricing for eggs. The dominating company is DANEGG (DANÆG), which has a market share of 70%. Due to its influential position, DANEGG sets the prices for the producers as well as the consumers. Thus, the company is in a perfect position to carry out a monopsonistic policy.

Fig. 10.1 illustrates the theory and compares it with DANEGG's actual policy.

AA is the expected demand curve for eggs. If we assume that the payment for eggs is the only cost, marginal cost equals the price paid to the producers. If the company wants to maximize profit it will equal marginal income and marginal cost; thus, the company's marginal income curve will be identical with the demand curve for the producers. The supply curve must be assumed to be increasing. Some producers have concentrated on eggs; for others it is only a little extra income. If the quoted price is too low, some producers will find it more remunerative to produce other goods. On the condition that all producers behave rationally, all will produce the quantity at which the price is equal to their individual marginal costs. Should the quoted price be p_1 the volume offered for sale will be m_1. If the company wants a higher volume, such as m_2, the price has to be increased to p_2. As the price p_2 also has to be paid for the eggs that would have been bought at price p_1, DANEGG's marginal cost curve must increase more than the supply curve from the producers. Thus, the optimum volume will be m_0, where DANEGG's marginal cost is equal to marginal income. The producers will be paid the price p_3, and the final consumers will be charged the price p_4.

This simplified theory has to be modified for various reasons. First, the company has other costs than the prices paid to the producers. This

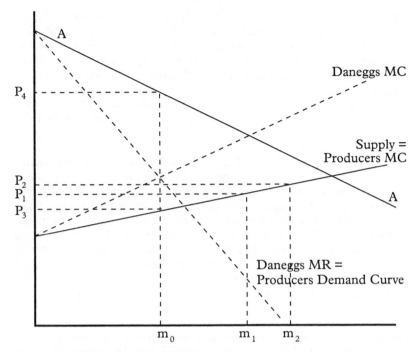

Figure 10.1 Optimal pricing for eggs

does not change the basic principles. Other costs simply have to be added to the marginal cost curve.

Second, DANEGG does not have an absolute monopoly. Thus, if the price to the producers is low, the competitors could offer a higher price, which would affect the supply to DANEGG.

Third, the exposition is based on the assumption that the company wants short-term profit maximization. If that is the case, prices can be squeezed to a level at which the producers can only cover their variable costs.

Fourth, it is a condition that no public authority intervenes and regulates prices.

Even though there are competitors, the relationship to each supplier is monopsonistic, at least in the short term, because the producer by contract is obligated to deliver to DANEGG only. But presented in its short-term version, the theory is definitely not relevant, for the simple reason that the goal is not short-term profit maximization. (The major reason for this is that DANEGG is a cooperative.) If the goal were profit maximization, DANEGG would import the eggs rather than buy them from Danish producers.

The company is not interested in any exploitation of the producers. In contrast, it wants the relationship to the producers to be such that it is guaranteed a steady supply. Management itself expresses its policy in the following terms: its primary concern is to secure constant deliveries. It is fully aware that most of the producers have alternatives. They can give up producing eggs or they can sell their eggs through other channels; what DANEGG is afraid of is not that the producers will sell to its competitors but that they will sell directly to the consumers (or local retailers). Management prefers to use the phrase that the price to the producers should be fair so that they are interested in continuing their deliveries.

The other example is the market for sugar. Danisco is the only manufacturer of sugar in Denmark. Consequently, as there is only one buyer of sugar beets, we have perfect monopsony. Growers can decide whether they want to grow sugar beets or other crops, but if they choose sugar beets they have no alternative but to sell them to Danisco. This situation is fairly recent. Until 1989 there was a competitor that offered some competition, also on price. But in that year it was acquired by Danisco. The following exposition relates to the present situation, but we shall give a few remarks on how the relations were before 1989.

Danisco's strategy towards the growers of sugar beets cannot be understood without rudimentary knowledge of the world market for sugar. Since 1967, the production of sugar has been regulated by the European Community. The regulation takes the form of quotas to each Member State, which implies a limitation on total production.[79]

The quota is divided into three parts. The basic quota is the A-quota, which corresponds to the European Community's own consumption. To give the most efficient producers the possibility for higher production, there is an additional B-quota. For A- and B-quotas, the European Community guarantees a minimum price. If the price obtained is lower than the guaranteed price, the European Community reimburses the price difference. If the price is higher, a tax has to be paid. This mechanism attempts to secure the same price for A and B sugar in the entire European Community. Extra production above the A and B quotas is termed C-sugar. It has to be exported outside the European Community at whatever price can be obtained, and there is no price guarantee. For Danisco, the basic income originates from the sale of A and B sugar, whereas C sugar is marginal because the price normally is lower.

How does this system influence the prices offered to the growers? Because of the regulation, the theory as illustrated in Figure 10.1 cannot be applied unmodified. There is no demand curve in the ordinary sense.

The regulatory system is directly reflected in the relationship to the growers of sugar beets. Contracts are made annually with the farmers and are also divided into A, B and C quotas. The price is highest for A

---

[79] The system is rather complicated. Here we have to concentrate on the basic principles and omit a number of details, even though they are relevant for the entire system of pricing.

and lowest for C. The prices are so advantageous that it nearly always pays to fulfill the A and B quotas. The reason why Danisco does not try to squeeze the price is the same as for eggs. If it should venture it one year, many growers would not dare to sign contracts the following year and the result would be disastrous. The firm's main concern is to ensure a steady supply of high-quality sugar beets. The chance for an extra short-term profit is not worth the risk.

The market for C-sugar is more like normal business, as the market is free. For this quota, Danisco applies a marginal way of reasoning right out of the textbook. Export prices vary but are normally lower than on the guaranteed market. Much effort is made to obtain a correct estimate of marginal costs. The prices for the sugar beets are pressed down, but it cannot be called exploitation, as few growers deliver more than their A and B quotas. But marginal manufacturing costs increase. With the beets come soil and dirt, and the more that is produced, the more the machines are worn out and have to be repaired. The result is that the utilization of the C-quotas is fairly small.

The relationships to the growers before 1989, when there was a competitor, were the same as now. There was active competition, but it did not manifest itself in the prices offered to the growers. Each of the companies had fixed contracts with the growers. But there was competition on sales prices. As mentioned in chapter 9, Danisco gives no discounts. But the competitor occasionally did. Thus, Danisco once became aware that one of its big customers obtained a (small) discount from its competitor. It reacted immediately and the threat of a local price war was sufficient.

We have only presented two cases. But other examples point in the same direction. Big and well known firms refrain from conspicuous exploitation of their monopsony power. They are interested in stable long-term relationships; are sensitive to their image; and want to avoid any form of government intervention.

10.3 Subcontracting

The theory of monopsony can also apply to a situation in which a *subcontractor* delivers its products to a single buyer.

Subcontracting has become more and more common, and many firms work exclusively as subcontractors. Usually the balance of power is not even. For a small company, there may be cost advantages in giving up its own market and instead focusing on the delivery of a highly specialized product to a single buyer. But the power resides with the buyer, and the subcontractor could find itself exploited and eventually forced to shut down, and the buyer then finds the next victim to take over the contract. But subcontractors are not defenseless. They may retain some production of their own. And for very special products, the buying company may be just as dependent on subcontractors as the subcontractors are on the company. The subcontractors may be in a situation in which they can press the price upwards with the threat of not delivering.

There are many examples of subcontractors suffering great losses, sometimes so great that they could not survive. But there are even more cases of stable and permanent relations.

As an illustrative example we select the experiences of a French chocolate manufacturer.[80] *Carrefour*, the biggest retail chain in France, is well known for its innovative ideas. One such idea, called *produits libres*, in other words products without a brand name, was introduced in the 1970s. These products were sold in normal supermarkets, but at a lower price than the well known brands. Carrefour asked its regular suppliers if they were interested in producing the nameless products along with their traditional brands. For example, Carrefour initially asked Nestlé if it would be interested in manufacturing chocolate *produits libres*. Nestlé declined the offer because they feared that such a move would be detrimental to its ordinary sales. As a result, Carrefour offered the contract to a small chocolate manufacturer in Toulouse whose brands were relatively unknown outside the local region. The manufacturer felt that there was a great deal of risk involved in producing the product but also a potentially high payoff. The manufacturer had to neglect its own brands, which could result in a loss of its own market. In addition, the manufacturer would become increasingly dependent on Carrefour, who could potentially force down the price to a point below the manufacturer's total average costs. This move would force the manufacturer out of business, and Carrefour would move to the next victim and repeat the process.

How likely is it that this would actually happen? The probability is extremely low, as this type of aggressive and exploitive use of power would give Carrefour a bad reputation in the European chocolate industry. This image would make it extremely difficult for Carrefour to find a new victim, and therefore, it is in Carrefour's best interest to ensure the manufacturer's survival. Hence the chocolate manufacturer may have real power by threatening to close down.

10.4 Relations between producers and retailers

Historically, retailers have enjoyed a relatively strong position; a local monopoly was typical in small communities, whereas a position of great influence was enjoyed by the retailers in the more competitive, larger communities. It was the retailer who chose which goods to carry and to recommend. This position began to diminish with the rise of heavily advertised brands and the introduction of self-service. Many brands became so popular that the retailer had to carry them and power began to shift from the retailer to the supplier. This balance of power shifted back

---

[80] Source: personal information from Carrefour.

to the retailers with the process of concentration that took place in retailing. The retail sector in Sweden has become so concentrated that only three retail chains dominate all household goods. This market structure makes it essential for manufacturers to have their products accepted by at least one of these retail organizations – and preferably all of them. Even a manufacturer that controls the strongest brands can no longer dictate trade conditions – including price – but rather must negotiate terms with the retail chains. Brand names still play a role, but a diminishing one, as an increasing number of lesser known products are sold in certain markets.

As the concentration process within retailing is much stronger for convenience goods than for speciality goods, the increase in retail power should be less pronounced for speciality shops. This point of view is clearly expressed by Michael Porter.[81]

When chain stores penetrate a given class of retail outlets, the number of buyers of a given product is reduced, and Porter hypothesizes that the manufacturers' return will decrease. This hypothesis is consistent with Ward's studies of retailing in the United Kingdom, where he finds for the 1960s that the rise of chains has reduced manufacturer margins.[82]

My own observations on the Danish market agree with this hypothesis. The strong chains for everyday goods exercise strong pressure on the manufacturers, but this is not the case for speciality shops.

A limited number of retailers may influence the manufacturers' return in other ways. Thus, Stigler postulates that the willingness of the manufacturer to make secret price concessions to retail buyers is lower when the number of retailers is high, because the probability of detection by rival manufacturers then will be higher.[83] Thus, a limited number of retailers may undermine oligopolistic consensus within manufacturing.

It is doubtful whether Danish experiences support this hypothesis. Thus, before the growth of the supermarket chains, when the number of retailers was great, the price structure for oleo-margarine gave practically all retailers an individual and secret discount. This is not the case now.

Although the supplier still sets the price, the buyer's role is no longer limited to the decision of how much to buy at the quoted price. The buyer and seller are both involved in negotiations on price and other trade conditions. These conditions can take several forms. For example, both parties may try to obtain a right of exclusivity; the sellers restrict the buyers so that they are unable to sell competing products, and the buyers restrict the sellers so that they do not supply their competitors.

---

[81] Michael Porter, *Interbrand choice, strategy, and bilateral market power*, 1976.

[82] T.S. Ward, "The distribution of consumer goods: structure and performance", 1973.

[83] See George Stigler, "A theory of oligopoly", *Journal of Political Economy*, 1964.

An example of an exclusive agreement is a situation in which the buyer has the exclusive right to a particular brand but not to other products. If a retailer's business is damaged by strong competition, it may seek assistance from its suppliers. Suppliers will often support the retailer by providing special discounts or possibly discontinuing deliveries to the competitors. Other means of assistance include: granting credit to the retailer, contributing to the sales effort and offering consultative services.

The market for *beer* in Denmark provides a good illustration of the development of trade relationships between an industry and its customers.

There are 12 breweries in Denmark; Carlsberg (which includes the Tuborg breweries) is the dominant firm, with a market share of 80%. Although Carlsberg's products have a strong market position, some of the smaller breweries have also obtained brand recognition, and a number of inexpensive brands have developed a limited market share.

Traditionally, the breweries delivered to the retailers through local depots. These depots had a monopoly of the brands within the local region. This system was suitable for supplying a large number of independent retailers, but not appropriate for delivery to the central warehouses of the large retail chains.

Industry pricing is based on an agreement generated by the brewers' association. This agreement states that there are fixed minimum prices for beer (with the exception of certain discount brands) – and that all types of discounts are prohibited. The agreement was structured to eliminate price competition within the trade. The traditional policy of the Carlsberg breweries has been the maintenance of peaceful relations within the industry. Carlsberg appears to have no desire to become a monopoly; it has not attempted to drive out the smaller breweries by initiating price wars; instead, it has assisted other breweries in various ways. Carlsberg has acquired shares in some of these breweries in order to expand its realm of influence. Carlsberg's traditional policy has been to charge at a fairly high level. One reason for this pricing policy is to give the smaller breweries, with relatively high costs, a chance to survive. Carlsberg has not always been able to maintain this high level policy, as it sometimes has been forced to compete on price against the inexpensive brands sold at discount prices.

Let us now turn to the vertical relations. This relationship remained harmonious as long as the retailers were taken care of by a number of small independent shops. However, this vertical harmony became threatened by the creation of strong chains, which posed a conflict of interest. These strong chains were not interested in the uniformity of beer prices. The first sign of conflict occurred during Christmas of 1984, when a chain of large discount stores sold Carlsberg beer at a price of DKK 98.95 for a case of 30 bottles. Shortly afterwards, another chain sold a case of beer for DKK 99.95. In both cases, the delivery price from the brewery was DKK 119.10. Carlsberg's response was to immediately stop delivery to the two chains.

Why did Carlsberg do this? The action of the two chains did not negatively impact Carlsberg's earnings. It obtained its normal level of profit and the discount policy could potentially have increased the brewery's total sales volume. Carlsberg had nothing to lose from the activities of the two chains. A possible explanation could be that the brewery was concerned that not all of the other retailers would be interested in promoting the sale of Carlsberg at discount prices and that some might actually boycott the beer. However, this is not really a viable concern, as retailers must carry the brands of the market leader in order to compete.

Carlsberg's management has cited recent industry trends as the reason for the firm's behavior. There has been a concentration of retailers during the last two or three decades, characterized by the disappearance of small sales outlets and the development of larger stores. This concentration implies that the balance of power between retailing and industry has shifted to the disadvantage of the Carlsberg breweries. Thus, in the long term, it is in Carlsberg's best interest to help the small retailers to survive. Carlsberg's attitude towards discounting will impact the policy's implementation within the industry. The breweries are not interested in providing any discounts that will benefit the large retail organizations.

A complex relationship exists between the pharmaceutical industry in Denmark and its customers, the pharmacists. The pharmacists seem to be in a strong position as they represent the only – or at least main – sales outlet for the industry's products. But it is primarily the doctors and not the pharmacists who decide which products are to be sold. Therefore the industry concentrates on winning the favor of the doctors, not the pharmacists. The relations are further complicated by the fact that the pharmacists simultaneously are the pharmaceutical industry's principal competitor and their main customer. Pharmacists rely on the industry to manufacture certain products but are capable of producing basic items in their own shop. The pharmacists often have an old pill-manufacturing machine and must choose between purchasing the pills externally or producing them.

The competition between the pharmacists and the pharmaceutical industry is interesting from an economic perspective. According to economic theory, the pharmacists should manufacture pills if their marginal costs are lower than the price they pay to the pharmaceutical companies. The pharmacist can make a reasonable estimate of marginal costs. The cost of the pill machine and the premises are both considered sunk costs. The best alternative use costs could be estimated for both of these factors, but this is a rather sophisticated approach for a pharmacist.

Wage costs are extremely important. If the production can take place during slack periods, then wage costs do not increase as a result of the manufacturing process. Marginal costs appear to be limited and include little more than materials.

Traditionally, pharmacists manufactured selected products. However, when volume dropped it became unprofitable to continue production, and the manufacturing process became concentrated at a few pharmacists who then distributed to others. This trend resulted in the establishment of the pharmacists' own production company.

The pharmaceutical industry employed a full cost pricing system and therefore, the pharmacists' production became a source of competition. The pharmaceutical industry complained to the National Board of Health, citing an unfair competitive action by the pharmacists, because the industry used full cost and the pharmacists a marginal approach. As a result, pharmacists were forced to adopt a full cost pricing policy. The National Board of Health made it mandatory for them to calculate overhead according to industry standards and wages according to a full cost method.

Thus, we have an example in which a public authority forced a trade to abandon marginal reasoning. Under a free market structure, the outcome would have been different.

11. Conclusion

The main topic has been the relationship between pricing in theory and pricing in practice. Students at universities and business schools are often critical towards the theory they learn, sometimes formulated that price theory is unrealistic. It is not always clear what they mean, but at least they feel that there is a discrepancy between theory and practice.

There are various reasons why it is difficult to give a precise answer to the question of whether there is harmony between theory and practice – or not. Practice is manifold. For a theory to be in accordance with practice, it must be sufficient that correspondence can be found in a substantial number of cases, because it is impossible for any theory to be in agreement with all practical examples of pricing.

So practice is not a clear-cut concept. But neither is theory. It is not relevant that the theory may be formulated by the use of total, average or marginal concepts, for basically they express the same line of thinking. Our attention has been focused on the theory formulated in marginal terms. What is relevant is that the theory may be based on different assumptions. Normally these are profit maximization, perfect information, no regulations – and *ceteris paribus* (all things being equal). Often the assumptions are further simplified: only the short term is considered, one single product is manufactured and so on. This is the way price theory is presented in most textbooks on managerial economics or the theory of pricing.

Of course such a theory is unrealistic, for the simple reason that these assumptions are never fulfilled in real life. But the theory can be expanded by modifying the assumptions and by constructing more complicated but also more realistic models. Instead of profit maximization, you can construct multi-goal models; and the single-product case may be replaced by a multi-product model.

A fundamental point is whether the condition of profit maximization is realistic. This assumption has often come under attack.

For the assumption to be an acceptable starting-point, it must be sufficient that profit is the normal goal; other goals may exist, but as modifications of the primary goal: profit. My point of view is that, if the theory is to be based on one single goal, it has to be profit maximization. It must be admitted that numerous modifications have to be made. Management in our days is often more concerned with growth, prestige and turnover; ethical considerations have an influence; and profit satisfaction may in many situations be more relevant than maximization. On the other hand, many companies have been forced to give priority to profit because margins have been squeezed to the point at which they have to get the best out of every bargain. Maximum profit may be synonymous with the ability to survive. The Danish publishing industry has been used as an example in the text. Traditionally, many publishers have had other motives than profit. But those that have neglected the importance of profit do not exist any more.

The absolute majority of price models are based on short-term profit maximization. Long-term maximization could presumably be expected to be more realistic. But the assumption of maximization in the short term is not irrelevant. It is surprising how often even big firms concentrate on solving the acute problems and neglect long-term effects. But still the main emphasis should be placed on the long term.

The distinction between normative and descriptive theory has been a main point in this book.

For a normative theory, the marginal way of thinking is realistic if it presents helpful guidance to the decision-maker. In my mind there is no doubt that the theory is useful. In numerous situations I have felt how the very logic of the theory presented a constructive way of thinking. But I am equally convinced that the theory often does more harm than good when the elementary models are applied in situations in which the assumptions are not fulfilled or when the theory is simply misunderstood. Thus, I have observed time after time that the requirements of price elasticity for a price reduction to be remunerative are underrated.

The normative marginal theory is invariably based on profit maximization – normally in the short term. In principle, it is perfectly possible to construct models based on other assumptions. The theory has developed multi-goal models. Such models are of limited interest, because other goals can rarely be stated sufficiently precisely for the models to be workable. The best procedure for solving a problem is to base the analysis on profit maximization, to determine an optimum price. But this analysis should not be understood as determining the end result, but as the starting-point for the final deliberations, in which other considerations are taken in as modifications.

Most students never get beyond the basic elementary models. Problems in practice are often so complicated that these models are not sufficient. A typical situation is that the correct decision depends on 10 different factors. But that is too complicated for the average decision-maker. They concentrate on 2 or 3 factors and neglect the others – with the obvious risk that they overlook an essential factor.

The elementary models therefore have to be extended. This makes them more correct, but also more complicated. There is a constant cry from practice for simplified models. It is sometimes formulated as follows: "You are right. We ought to take all relevant factors into consideration. But then it could take 6 months before we can make a decision. We must apply a simplified way of reasoning – even though it sometimes leads to mistakes."

Economic theory can be criticized for having neglected this point. It has concentrated on constructing more and more sophisticated models, which are perfectly logical but of little practical use. The models are based on full information, but this condition is seldom fulfilled in practice. What practice needs is guidance on how to apply the theoretical models under imperfect information. It might even be a job for economists to construct rules of thumb that are not logical but are superior to those that industry itself has developed.

Theory has made progress on other points. Most important is the construction of simulation models. Many important decisions in the future will be based on computer technology. But the majority of decisions will still be made by more simplified methods.

The second question of whether marginal theory can be used as a descriptive theory is more complicated. What is the criteria for agreement between theory and practice? Is it the way of reasoning that is relevant or is it the result? The decision-makers may use perfect marginal reasoning but may not arrive at an optimum solution because of imperfect information. Or they may reason along lines that have not the slightest resemblance to marginal theory, but afterwards it can be demonstrated that the price is the optimum one. This correspondence may be *ex post* and not *ex ante*. In the same moment the price is set, consumers may accept it as a normal price and may react against a price increase, even though they would have been willing to pay that price *ex ante*. A perfect statistical analysis might afterwards be able to prove that marginal cost equals marginal revenue, thus leading to the conclusion that the actual price is in agreement with the marginal theory, a conclusion that is misleading.

The requirement for a descriptive theory is that it be able to explain the pricing process. Not in all details, but in broad lines. But the theory also must be able to make predictions, such as the effect on prices of increased wages, changes in demand, imposition of a unit tax and so on.

Let us start with our conclusion: *marginal theory is not acceptable as a general descriptive theory*. The theory is normally applied in its simplified, short-term version. Take the welfare theory as an illustrative example. Most of this theory has as its foundation that existing firms have set their prices so that the marginal cost equals the marginal revenue. But observations seem to indicate a systematic tendency for prices to be lower than the short-term optimum. Thus, the entire welfare theory is based on unrealistic assumptions. That is not tantamount to saying that welfare theory is without value. Its relevance consists in its systematic analysis of essential problems. It is like building more and more elegant ivory towers on a shaky foundation. The short-term theory is too simplified to be acceptable as a general theory, as so many other important factors play a role.

The obvious solution is to elaborate the simple theory into a more realistic but more complicated theory. This can be done by including more relevant factors and by accepting long-term instead of short-term maximization. But the inevitable result is that precision is lost. In an elaborated theory a firm is not confronted with one demand curve (and correspondingly one marginal revenue curve). There are many: a short-term function versus a function in which consumers have had time to adjust their buying habits. One curve is based on the assumption of no competitor reaction and others on various assumptions of competitor behavior. One is based on no government interference; others foresee different types of regulation. Correspondingly, cost curves may be interpreted as applying to the short or the long term. Thus, there is not one optimum price. There are a multitude.

This is a minor problem for the normative theory. For it is the decision-makers who makes the choice of assumptions. They decide whether to focus on the short or the long term. But a descriptive theory is different. It is a theory developed by outsiders, and how can outsiders know whether short- or long-term considerations are relevant? And how can they know whether the goal is profit maximization or something else?

Thus, even for the more elaborated versions of the marginal theory, it is doubtful to what extent the theory at its present stage is adequate as a descriptive theory. There are numerous cases of prices that agree with the theory, but the exceptions are many. So many that the predictive value of the theory is low.

As the marginal theory does not seem adequate as a descriptive theory, it is natural to look for alternatives.

Through time, some economists have proposed alternatives that can all be grouped under the heading of full cost. These theories are characterized by explaining the pricing process exclusively by cost factors. But a full cost theory is even less acceptable than marginal theory. The theory may be in accordance with actual pricing within special fields, but it can never be accepted as a general theory for the obvious reason that it entirely neglects demand factors. A full cost theory can explain certain phenomena, but there are more observations that can never find their explanation in cost fact ors alone.

Thus, the conclusion is that, at its present stage, economics is not able to offer any realistic descriptive theory. But this situation is not acceptable for any science!

We have to realize that the pricing process is so manifold that no theory will ever do as a general theory – if it has to be simple. But if it is extended by including all imaginable relevant factors it becomes unworkable.

There is no easy solution.

Parts of the traditional theory are characterized by not giving precise conclusions but only stating possibilities. Take the oligopoly theory as a clear example. The theory limits itself to enumerating different possibilities, but the theory itself can hardly be used to predict what will happen in a given situation. You can expand the theory of oligopoly by constructing models under more and more complicated assumptions. But that will not help. We will have to make systematic observations of how oligopolists behave in different situations. On this basis we may venture a prediction that oligopolists normally will act in this and this way. And we can improve the value of prediction by studying individual oligopolists and say that, based on existing evidence, they are likely to do so and so in the present situation.

Thus, we have to realize that no single theory can explain everything. The solution must be to establish a form of typology. This typology should state under which conditions different types of models are realistic. Thus, to use one of our examples: in the publishing industry, a price model stating that price depends on the category of book, number of pages and number of copies printed can explain actual pricing – and may even be able to predict what the price of a forthcoming book is likely to be. In contrast, the marginal theory has no chance of reliably estimating what the price of a book will be.

With all its defects, the marginal theory still seems the best choice for a descriptive theory. But its shortcomings must be made clear, and amendments and improvements have to be made:

- The assumption of profit maximization is not always relevant. Thus, if it seems likely in a certain situation that an alternative goal is relevant, another model has to be used, for example, a model based on maximum turnover under certain profit restraints.

- The theory concentrates on determining the optimum price. Not necessarily so in practice. Normally any approximation is acceptable to management. The concept of a fair price may play a role. Imagine a situation in which it is evident that the demand for a product has increased to the extent that capacity is fully utilized. The marginal theory would predict that a price increase will occur in the nearest future. But the prediction is likely to be wrong. If profit is satisfactory and the price considered as fair, it may very well remain unaltered.

- Uncertainty plays a great role in practice. Hence theories dealing with imperfect information, uncertainty and other factors are relevant.

- The separation of costs into variable and fixed costs is useful in elementary models. But it is a primitive distinction. In numerous situations in practice, the cost structure is so complicated that applying this simplified distinction is misleading. This is more relevant for the normative than the descriptive theory.

- There is a strong tradition in elementary as well as advanced textbooks for drawing demand curves as straight lines. When the only relevant fact is that the demand curve slopes downward, you might as well make it a straight line. In the real world, demand curves are never straight. This can create problems, as reasoning based on straight lines may lead to false conclusions.

References

Andrews, P.W.S., *Manufacturing Business*, Macmillan, London, 1949.

Atkin, B and Skinner, R., *How British Industry Prices. Industrial Market Research*, 1975.

Bain, Joe, *Price Theory*, New York: Holt & Co., 1952.

Barback, R.H., *The Pricing of Manufacturers*, Macmillan, London, 1964.

Baumol, W.J., *Business Behaviour*, Value and Growth, New York, 1967.

Benvignati, Anita M., "An Empirical Investigation of International Transfer Price by U.S. Manufacturing Firms", in Rugman and Eden, *Multinationals and Transfer Pricing*, New York, 1985.

Call, Steven and Holahan, William, *Microeconomics*, Belmont, California: Wadsworth Publishing Company, 1983.

Carlton D.W., "Contracts, Price Rigidity and Market Equilibrium", *Journal of Political Economy*, October 1979, Vol. 87, pp. 1038-1058.

Caves, R.E, Porter M.E. and Spencer, A.M., *Competition in the Open Economy*, Cambridge, Mass.: Harvard University Press, 1980.

Cooper, R and Kaplan, R.S., "How Cost Accounting Distorts Product Costs", *Management Accounting*, April, p.20-27, 1988.

Cooper, R and Kaplan, R.S., "Measure Costs Right. Make the Right Decisions", *Harvard Business Review*, No. 5, September-October 1988.

Dean, Joel, *Managerial Economics*, Prentice-Hall, Englewood Cliffs, New Jersey, 1951.

Dorward, Neil, *Pricing Decision*, London: Harper & Row, 1987.

Douglas, E.J., *Managerial Economics, Theory, Practice and Problems*, Englewood Cliffs, 1983.

Earley, J.S., "Marginal Policies of Excellently Managed Companies", *American Economic Review*, 1956, pp. 44-70.

Eccles, R.G., "Control with Fairness in Transfer Pricing", *Harvard Business Review*, Vol. 61, No. 6, 1983, pp. 149-161.

Edwards, H.R., Competition and Monopoly in the British Soap Industry, Clarendon Press, Oxford. 1962.

Eiteman, W.J., *Price Determination. Business Practice versus Economic Theory*, Ann Arbor, 1949.

Friedman, J.W., *Oligopoly Theory*, Cambridge University Press, 1983.

Gabor, Andre, *Pricing. Principles and Practices*, London, 1980.

Geroski, P., Phlips, L. and Ulph, A., "Oligopoly, Competition and Welfare", *Journal of Industrial Economics*, 1985, pp. 369-86.

Gordon, Robert, "Output Fluctuations and Gradual Price Adjustment", *Journal of Economic Literature*, Vol. XIX, June 1981, pp. 493-530.

Hague, D.C., *Pricing in Business*, George Allen & Unwin, 1971.

Haynes, Warren, Pricing Decisions in Small Business, University of Kentucky Press, Lexington, 1962.

Hirshleifer, Jack, *Price Theory and Applications*, Prentice Hall, Englewood Cliffs, N.J., 1984.

Hirshleifer, Jack, "On the Economics of Transfer Pricing", *Journal of Business*, Vol. XXIX, July 1956, pp. 172-84.

Kaplan, A.D.H., Dirlam, J.B and Lanzilotti, R.F., *Pricing in Big Business*, Washington D.C.: Brookings Institute, 1958.

Kaplan, R.S., "The Evolution of Management Accounting", *The Accounting Review*, Vol. LIX, July 1984, pp. 390-418.

Koutsoyiannis, A., *Modern Microeconomics*, London: Macmillan, 1975.

Kreps, D.M. and Schenkman, J.A., "Quantity Precommitment and Bertrand Competition Yield. Cournot Outcomes", *Bell Journal of Economics*, Vol. 14, No. 2, 1983, p. 326-337.

Lee, Frederic S., "The Marginalist Controversy and the Demise of Full Cost Pricing", *Journal of Economic Issues*, Vol. XVIII, No. 4, December 1984.

Machlup, F., "Marginal Analysis and Empirical Research", *American Economic Review*, Vol. XXXVI, No. 4, September 1946, pp. 519-54.

Marshall, Arthur, *More Profitable Pricing*, McGraw Hill, London, 1980.

Monroe, Kent B., *Pricing. Making Profitable Decisions*, McGraw Hill Publishing Company, New York, 1990 (second edition).

Montgomery Cynthia A. and Wernerfelt, Birger, "Diversification, Ricardian Rents and Tobins q", *Rand Journal of Economics*, 1988.

Mulvihill, Donald F and Paranha, Stephen, *Price Policies and Practices*, New York, 1967.

Oxenfeldt, Alfred R., *Pricing Strategies*, Amacon, New York, 1975.

Phlips, L., *The Economics of Price Discrimination*, Cambridge: Cambridge University Press, 1983.

Phlips, L., *Predatory Pricing*, Luxembourg, 1987.

Porter, Michael E., *Interbrand Choice, Strategy and Bilateral Power*, Cambridge, Mass., 1976.

Porter. Michael E., *Competitve Strategy*, New York: Free Press, 1980.

Radner, Roy, "Collusive Behavior in Non-Cooperative Epsilon-. Equilibria of Oligopolists with Long but Finite Lives", *Journal of Economic Theory*, No. 2, April 1980, pp.136-154.

Scherer, F. M., *Industrial Pricing Policies*, Chicago, Ill, 1970.

Shipley, D.D., "Pricing Objectives in British Manufacturing Industry", *Journal of Industrial Economics*, Vol. XXIX, No. 4, June 1981, pp. 429-43.

Shubik, M., *Strategy and Market Structure*, John Wiley, 1959.

Silberston, "Surveys of Applied Economics: Price Behaviour of Firms", *Economic Journal*, Vol. LXXX, September 1970, pp. 511 – 572.

Simon. H., "Pricing opportunities – And How to Exploit Them", *Sloan Management Review*, Vol. 33, No. 2, 1992, pp. 55-65.

Skinner, R.C., "The Determination of Selling Prices", *Journal of Industrial Economics*, Vol. XVIII, No. 3, July 1970, pp. 201-17.

Stigler G.J., "A Theory of Oligopoly", *Journal of Political Economy*, 1964, pp. 44-61.

Sylos-Labini, P., "Industrial Pricing in the United Kingdom", *Cambridge Journal of Economics*, Vol. 3, No.2, June 1979, pp. 153-63.

Watson, I.R., *Pricing and Scale in Australian Industry*, Melbourne: AIDA Research Center, 1978.

Watson, D.S. and Getz, M., *Price Theory and Its Uses*, Boston: Houghton Miffin Co., 1981.

Weston. J.F., "Pricing Behavior of Large Firms", *Western Economic Journal*, 1972, pp. 1-16.

Wied-Nebbeling, S., *Industrielle Preissetzung*, Tübingen, 1975.

Winkler, John, *Pricing for Results*, Heineman Professional Publishing, Oxford, 1989.

Zajac. Edward E., *Fairness or Efficiency*, Cambridge. Mass. 1978.

Index

A
Activity-based costing 34
Annual bonus 143

B
Bertrand, Joseph 102
Boyer & Moreaux 104
Breweries 142, 154

C
Carrefour 152
Coffee, pricing of 49
Collusion 94, 102, 108
Cost accounting method 33
Cournot 10, 102, 113

D
Department stores 108, 111, 146
Detergent industry 27, 98, 104, 108, 111, 141
Discounting 50, 116, 143

E
Eccles, Robert C. 130
Efficient prices 81
Eggs, pricing of 148
Electrochemical industry 30
Ethical points of view 62, 126

G
Game theory 105
Goldsmiths 72, 112
Government investigations 12

H
Hirshleifer, Jack 101, 132
Hotel business 64, 70

J
Joint production 119

K
Kaplan, R. S. 34
Koutsoyiannis, A. 63, 74

M
Machlup, F. 73
McGuigan and Moyer 91
Medical industry 46, 55, 96, 108, 111
Multiple products 124

N
Newspaper 26, 49, 95, 104, 110

O
Oil refinery 121

P
Paint and dyestuff industry 69, 76
Papandreou, A.G. 79
Pareto optimum 81, 83
Personal interviews 12
Pharmaceutical industry 155
Porter, Michael 153
Poultry stations 122
Predatory pricing 140
Price discrimination 40, 48, 139
Price leadership 94
Pricing in restaurants 72
Printing industry 89, 157
Profit maximization 19, 43, 57, 105, 157, 161
Publishing houses 66, 87, 108, 146

Q
Quantity discount 143
Questionnaires 12, 75

R
Radner, Roy 103
Ramsey pricing 82

Regression technique 13
Restaurants 126
Retailers 152
Retailing 32, 49, 50, 116, 153
Rules of thumb 70, 77, 85, 112, 121, 125
Rush order 146

S
Saravia de la Calle, Luis 79
Scherer, F.M. 109
Scientific Pricing 92
Statistical analysis 13, 74
Stigler, George 153
Subcontracting 151

Subsidize 26, 54, 98
Sugar, pricing of 117, 150

T
Taxes 51, 135
Technical approach 32
Tivoli amusement park 39

V
Value-added tax (VAT) 53

W
Welfare theory 81